Home Light

John Booth

Copyright © 2015 John Booth

All rights reserved, including the right to reproduce this book, or portions thereof in any form. No part of this text may be reproduced, transmitted, downloaded, decompiled, reverse engineered, or stored, in any form or introduced into any information storage and retrieval system, in any form or by any means, whether electronic or mechanical without the express written permission of the author.

The views expressed in this work are solely those of the author and do not necessarily reflect the views of the publisher, and the publisher hereby disclaims any responsibility for them.

Front cover design: copyright John Booth
Ordnance Survey map: "This work is based on data provided through www.VisionofBritain.org.uk and uses historical material which is copyright of the Great Britain Historical GIS Project and the University of Portsmouth."
Geological survey maps: U.S. Geological Survey, Department of the Interior/USGS.

ISBN: 978-1-326-29492-2

PublishNation, London
www.publishnation.co.uk

for Charlene

Introduction

If I'd known what was about to happen to me in the next four days I'd have made other plans. I'd have taken myself to hospital sooner, asked the nurses to keep an eye on me, leave the door open, that sort of thing. Anything to avoid the inevitable collision I was heading towards. But I hadn't a clue I was about to embark on the weirdest, most unimaginable journey ever. No way of knowing the final frontier was coming my way.

Some people say space is the final frontier. Well, space has its own place, along with time in our ever-present space-time continuum. Space goes on forever and ever and the further you go the more of it there is to find. I used to think that was the way it was. Over one horizon there's always another waiting to be crossed. But is it really like that? Not from where I'm now standing. If I could travel to the end of the universe faster than the speed of light I'd probably arrive at the beginning of time before I got to the end of space. And that's one of the biggest mysteries of our space-time continuum: why we can't have one without the other.

According to Einstein, time exists so that everything in space doesn't happen all at once. I sometimes think only he understands where I'm coming from and where I went. My question, the one that's occupied me for the last five years, is where exactly do you go when you leave the space-time continuum? And what happens if you come back? How do you fit the pieces back together?

Einstein reckons that the distinction between past, present and future is simply a stubbornly persistent illusion. Compared with the god of twentieth century physics, I know nothing. I'm a dumb fool. But in my case, this stubbornly persistent illusion unravelled. My geography and history, my own personal capsule of space and time, disappeared and I discovered that space wasn't the final frontier.

Before all this, I'd always imagined that death is the only thing in life that is final, but as it turned out it's not anything like I expected.

On the bus

It's Friday, March 8th, 1974. I'm seventeen, crowding through the gates of Kingston Grammar School, itching to get on with the weekend. 'Into the Mystic' off Van Morrison's new live album is playing in my head. A-levels are three months away and this is one of the last weekends I'll be allowed out before revision nails us to our desks; one of my last chances to catch up with Jenny.

As we exit the gates, my mate Nick gives me a shoulder punch, "You going down the Brewers tonight?"

"Yeah, and you?"

"Be there around eight."

"Do you know if Jenny's going to be there?"

Nick frowns like it's none of my business, "Guess so," he replies. I can tell he's hiding something, just not what it is. We've been best mates since we started junior school aged six, we both passed the 11-plus, the only two in our junior school to get scholarships for grammar school and we both have a passion for archaeology: we used to go on digs in the weekends. But now we're in our late teens we share fewer and fewer things in common and I can't tell why he's being cagey.

We're from the boys' school. Jenny and her girlfriends are from the girls' school. The Jolly Brewers is one of the few places we can meet: neutral ground down a cul-de-sac in the back-end of town. The only pub that will serve us a pint before we've turned eighteen. It's where we plan the weekend, find parties and gigs, drink beer, smoke cigarettes and practise with girls.

I'm in love with Jenny like only a seventeen year old can be. I can't get her out of my head. She's sweet sixteen, and beautiful even in a sulk which is a lot of the time. Tall and slim with long dark hair, styled hippie chic and big green eyes that light up when she smiles. I'm hoping this is the night I'll make my move, though I haven't a clue what I'll do. I want her to fall into my arms, but like Einstein says, gravity is not responsible for people falling in love. So how it'll pan out is a mystery. All I know is I want it to be proper romantic.

From the way Jenny stares at me across the bar or turns up at my side; the way she laughs at my jokes, flicks her hair or walks off in a huff, I reckon she feels the same. We're flirting with our future possibilities.

What I don't know is that my own future is threatened by a distinct lack of possibility. And the part Jenny might play as my life unravels is a mystery. And another thing, while I'm fixating on her, I'm too dim to notice she's playing the field, scouting her options, flirting with each of us in turn.

So with Jenny and the Brewers on my mind, I'm in a rush to get home, ditch the school uniform and get back to Kingston on the bus.

I tell Nick, "See you in the Brewers around eight."

"Yeah OK and then on to the Kaleidoscope?" he asks.

The Kaleidoscope Club is the after-hours community centre run by the local vicar. No alcohol allowed. Coffee and tea through a service hatch at five pence a plastic cup. Floor cushions to sit on and dope smoke wafting in the low lighting. It's where we end up after closing time with Jenny and her girlfriends. Where I hope to make my move.

We set off in different directions. I live a forty-five minute bus ride away. As I round the corner by the railway station, a 65 is stopped at the traffic lights. If the lights stay red and I run, there's a good chance of catching it. They only come every half hour and I don't have time to wait.

*

The way it is, most of my life so far has been a waiting game. Waiting for the minute hand to hit the hour, for the bell to ring, waiting for the bus, for the weekend, for something to happen. And while I'm waiting, my life doesn't belong to me. It's all about doing what I'm told by teachers and parents. They've mapped out my whole life while I'm not looking. I can't wait to finish school, leave home and win my freedom.

I'm studying History, Geography and English Literature. Past events, places I've never been and other people's stories, the world in someone else's book. At school that's all there is to life: the inside of a book; soaking up other people's facts and opinions; never being asked about my own. But the real world isn't in books. The real world is outside the school gates.

Playing guitar in our band, hiring rehearsal studios where no one's going to complain about the volume. Our stars are Hendrix, Zeppelin, Little Feat and Zappa – we're all convinced we're going to make it big. Going to gigs, parties, competing with mates – for the funniest stories, the misadventures, the best jokes, and girls. Looking for those places we can make our own – up in the trees in Bushy Park looking down on the world below, drinking in The Jolly Brewers, hanging out with people like us. This is the real world. And it doesn't come cheap. I have a Saturday job feeding the dishwashers in the Silver Café in Bentalls Department store and I work for my Dad: evenings, weekends and holidays. Whenever he needs my help converting one of his big Victorian houses into bed-sits to let to students: sawing, screwing, lifting, shovelling, plumbing, wiring, sanding, painting. You name it; I've done it. I've worked for him since I could first hold a hammer.

I reckon the way I feel most of the time is the same for all of us at that age. I'm invincible. I'm the centre of my own universe, bursting with energy and looking forward to my life ahead. It's not like I'm going to step off the platform to prove it but I'm pretty sure nothing can touch me.

*

If I knew what was around the corner I'd be paying more attention to the signs: a shortness of breath, a headache that comes and goes and a dull ache in my stomach for the last couple of weeks; things I put down to exam pressure. The symptoms started after a flu that kept me out of school and in bed for a week on honey and lemon, popping eight aspirins a day, my mother's cure-all.

I'd thrown a whitey visiting two of my mates in hospital. They were in traction after a serious bike crash. Seeing blood-soaked bandages wrapped round steel pins in their legs, the ward started to spin. I reached for something solid to ground myself, grabbed a trolley on wheels, it spun round too and landed me on the floor.

My mother said "You've always been queasy about blood," and we thought nothing of it. Then it happened again, practising for my driving test. The world closed in, my hands became rubber and I almost blacked out. As the car weaved across the road towards some parked cars my mother took the wheel. She shouted, "What the devil are you playing at?"

"I feel faint."

"Well if I hadn't grabbed the wheel we would have crashed. Get out. I'm driving home." These were early warning signs of the trouble I was in but no one was paying attention, least of all me. I carry on regardless.

As it happens, there's an eight-foot skeleton cloaked in a black cowl, carrying a razor sharp scythe waiting patiently over my shoulder. He's got all the time in the world and only he knows I haven't. If I'd been raised in an old religion like my mother, I might have had a nagging suspicion that Death is always biding his time just behind me. But I wasn't raised in any religion and the only direction I'm looking is forwards.

I've learnt in school that the Grim Reaper first appeared in mythology as Charon, the ferryman. A skeletal body covered by a black cloak who ferries souls across the rivers of Hades. I guess that's how these things work in religions. Mythological figures get passed down from one tradition to the next, reappearing in different guises through the centuries. I believe in the Grim Reaper as much as I believe in Charon and his ferry: not at all.

The thing is, I'm an atheist. Taking after my father, my point of view is scientific. Cause and effect rule my world. All the stuff in the world, from us to the universe, is made of carbon atoms, the unchangeable building blocks of everything from macro to micro. We're all the sum of our parts from molecules to genes to cells.

Aside from being a landlord, my Dad is a biologist: a mycologist to be precise. He's an expert on fungi, the body of life that's neither plant nor animal but more common than either. He's raised my older sister and me to question everything scientifically. Anything that can't be proved empirically by many observers repeating the same experiments and producing the same results simply doesn't exist. I'm a confirmed empiricist. Science will undoubtedly solve all the mysteries of birth, life and death, probably in my lifetime. For us empiricists it's just a matter of time.

My father's definition of death – the one I've signed up for – is this: the heart stops pumping, the body dies, the brain switches off. Nothing more, nothing less. No Grim Reaper, no Charon, no rivers in Hades. I expect nothing. The lights will go out and that'll be it. Fungi will do the rest. Life is simply a biological process.

I like the biologist's point of view. Seeing as our atoms can neither be created nor destroyed they return to the soil or go up in smoke to be recycled into other life forms. To me, this sounds a bit like reincarnation; a biologist's version of reincarnation. Our atoms restart the slow climb up through all the biological life forms until finally some of them are reincarnated into other human beings, though it takes them a long time to do this. Atoms are so laid back.

We all have the atoms of the long dead inside us, like Shakespeare and Julius Caesar but none of the recent like Ghandi or Jimi Hendrix. Their atoms simply haven't had time to catch up.

The important distinction for us empiricists when it comes to reincarnation is that no matter how quickly or slowly our atoms recycle, they aren't going to take us along with them. Consciousness ceases, kaput. We live. We die. It's that's simple. I find that consoling. Nothing to fear in the end except the method and I guess we all hope we'll die peacefully in our sleep. How wrong can I be?

*

The lights stay red. I run for the bus. Fifty yards from the bus my heart goes into overdrive. Beating behind my eyeballs. Something's wrong. I'm slowing down. My vision's clouding over. I'm falling in slow motion. I'm on my knees, gasping for air and then flat out on the pavement. There are bugs crawling through a landscape of dirt trapped between the paving stones in front of my eyes and for some reason I find this fascinating. My heart is pounding in my chest, there's a rushing noise in my ears and I've got a throbbing headache. No point trying to get up, I know I can't.

All I can see of other pedestrians are their legs rushing past and I think *I'll just lie here on the pavement watching these legs walk past*. It seems like a normal thing to do. I'm in a bad way but I don't want to admit it, as if denying how I feel will make things better. I've learnt to ignore problems in the hope that they'll go away. Not causing a fuss is one of the cornerstones of my upbringing.

"There's always someone worse off than you, you know", that's my mother speaking in my head. And if she doesn't launch into her own miserable childhood or the inhabitants of the sinkhole council estates where she does her health visits it's "Count yourself lucky you're not a starving Biafran in Nigeria." So I don't call out for help.

If I lie here for long enough I'm sure someone will stop but everyone's caught up in their own business. I feel invisible. It's not as if passers-by can't see a teenager in his school uniform lying on the pavement in his black blazer, red and blue stripped tie, grey jumper. I don't look like a tramp, but people are too busy to stop.

After what seems like ages, but is probably only a minute or two, my heart starts to slow down. I catch my breath and my head stops throbbing. A woman leans over me, "Are you alright, can I help?" She's nice. "I only live round the corner, do you want to come and wait while I call an ambulance."

How I wish I'd let her call an ambulance. But I don't want to cause a fuss. It's going to mean doctors and hospitals and my mother complaining about what a lot of trouble I cause her, "Sometimes I think you're more trouble than you're worth," I can hear her already. And I've got better plans than hospitals; plans for tonight. If I can just get up I'm sure I'll soon feel better. So I look up at the nice woman and say, "No thanks, I'm alright, I must have tripped," and look round for a wonky paving stone I can blame for my fall.

"Are you sure?" she asks, not believing me.

"Yes, I feel fine," I lie and, noticing an uneven paving slab, mutter "Look, that's what did it." I drag myself up and brush myself off as if to prove I really am all right. The woman looks at me quizzically. She can tell I'm faking. I say, "My stop is just there, thank you for your help," and stumble to the bus stop holding my case under my arm.

I sit down on a low wall. Another bus pulls up, I get on. I climb the stairs to the top deck, carefully one by one, taking my time. I slump into my favourite seat at the back. Normally this is when I take off tie and blazer, so no one can identify which school I come from, and light up. But today a cigarette is the last thing on my mind.

I'm feeling a little better. I reckon I'm going to be all right. I count my pulse against the second hand on my watch. It's fast, about as fast as when I've just finished a hundred metre race in the pool. Swimming is my favourite sport – my only sport since I started winning galas for the school. I have to train four times a week to keep my place in the team so I reckon I must be fit. But my strength has disappeared.

The bus trundles past rows of boarded up shops. Every day the recession gets deeper. Garages are running out of petrol, capitalism is grinding to a halt. In January, the Tories announced the three-day working week, shutting Britain down because there isn't enough electricity to go round. The lights are going out across the country and half the week I revise by candlelight. We pass the Hawker Siddeley plane factory. Two sleek grey Harrier jump jets are parked on display in the forecourt, the latest in vertical take-off attack aircraft. I think it ironic that in the middle of a recession the armaments business is booming, but there's always a war on somewhere. Then we're in Ham, passing the butchers, the post office, the newsagents and F.W. Paine, the undertaker. Richmond Park drifts by, the bus climbs the hill past my favourite view of the water meadows on the banks of the Thames.

Teenagers from other schools are getting on and off the bus. Smokers crowd in the back of the upper deck. My head's swimming. I want to tell someone how I feel, just in case I keel over in my seat but I don't know how to do this. I mean, people don't talk to strangers on buses, unless they're an old biddy halfway to the loony bin.

Eventually, we pull up at my stop. I climb down the stairs and step off the gantry on to solid ground but the pavement is spongy and the street pulses in time to my heartbeat. My stomach hurts and my head's exploding.

I let myself into the house and drag my feet upstairs, one by one, resting every few steps to catch my breath like a wheezing old man. I crash out on my bed in my clothes and shoes and doze off waiting for my parents to return from work. I can't call them, don't have their work numbers and anyway, the phone's downstairs.

My mother wakes me and asks what on earth I'm doing on the bed in my school uniform. The uniform seems to matter more to her than the state I'm in, like she'll have to iron out the creases. I tell her how I collapsed and how my head and stomach hurt. My mother used to be a nurse, then a midwife and now she's a health visitor, so she takes it in her stride. She counts my pulse: it's racing; she goes to call the doctor's surgery in Kingston where she works.

Returning with a jug of water and a thermometer she says it's too late to go to the surgery this evening, back in Kingston, and it's too far for the doctor to come for a home visit, so she's decided we'll go tomorrow. My father comes up to commiserate. I'm not running a temperature but I'm too weak to get up so I stay in bed, eat some soup and curse my bad luck. This is the night I was going to tell Jenny how I feel about her.

I have a turntable by my bedside. I pull myself up on my elbow, put on Hendrix, *Electric Ladyland,* and drift off to 'Rainy Day, Dream Away'. I wake in the night to the sound of the needle clicking on the final groove. I reach for the off switch and stare at the ceiling in the light of the street lamps outside, wondering what's going on with me. I don't feel as invincible as I usually do and I'm no longer at the centre of my own universe. I've been displaced.

Drowning

Saturday, we drive back to Kingston to the doctor's surgery. The drive takes forever – me shifting in the passenger seat holding my belly, not able to find a comfortable spot. The doctor counts my racing pulse, takes some blood, prods my stomach where it hurts and scratches his head. He can't reach a diagnosis and recommends I'm admitted to hospital while we wait for the blood test results.

The pain is getting worse. I've changed my mind about going to hospital. I want to go straight there, right away. Whatever's wrong I'm sure the doctors can make it right. But my mother thinks differently. She's knows the way these things work, seeing as she's attached to our doctors' practice as a health visitor. She decides the hospital doctors won't be able to do any more than wait for the results.

So we go home.

Back in my bedroom, getting out of bed is becoming harder. My heart bangs away in my head. But whatever's the matter with me, it can't be life threatening. If it was, I feel sure my parents would be taking it more seriously.

Sunday, the doctor phones the results to my mother. My haemoglobin, the number of red blood cells in my bloodstream, is seven when it should be fifteen. He's arranged for a consultant to come and see me first thing Monday morning.

Now I know it's serious. Consultants don't normally make house calls. The day takes forever to pass. I've so little energy that I just lie there. I haven't a TV set or a radio to pass the time and I'm too exhausted to change records on the turntable.

Monday morning, mother tells me to get dressed while she waits downstairs for the consultant. She's in awe of consultants from her nursing days and wants to keep up appearances. I collapse on the floor trying to get changed but for the sake of appearances manage to pull my underpants and trousers on and get my arms inside a shirt and button it before dragging myself back onto the bed. I lie there fully clothed, feeling ridiculous. I should be in my pyjamas.

The consultant prods my stomach and asks me if I've seen any blood in my stools. I have to think for a second what my stools are and when I realise I say no, I haven't, although they've been dark recently like when you drink red wine. I'm white as a sheet and he tells me I'm seriously anaemic.

Before he leaves he uses our phone and arranges for me to be admitted to hospital. He asks my mother to call an ambulance. An ambulance is what I need. I'm so weak I want to be carried down the stairs on a stretcher. But my mother thinks we can get to the hospital quicker in her car. I've been lying in bed for two days waiting for something to happen, so I don't understand why we're now in such a rush. Mother and me stumble down the stairs together, she can't take my weight and as I hang on to the banister to stop us falling, I wrench my stomach.

In the hospital they give me a room to myself on the ground floor with a view of a beautiful garden. It's a sunny spring day. At last I feel safe, I'm in the best place I can be in the circumstances. A doctor examines me, prods my stomach where it hurts. He doesn't know the cause and schedules tests.

Mother fills out forms with work numbers, addresses and so on, then leaves for work. She has an antenatal class of expectant mothers to go to and she says she can't let them down. I reckon that's why we were in such a rush. A nurse comes in and asks if I want some lunch. I'm not hungry but she thinks I need to eat so I have some tomato soup.

After lunch I drift restlessly, half awake, half asleep. I'm in a daze. Time passes.

I come to, bile rising in my throat. I throw up over the sheets. At first I think it's the tomato soup but then it dawns on me it's blood. I shout for a nurse. Nurses arrive and clean me up, change the sheets and while that's happening a doctor arrives. He thinks I've got a burst stomach ulcer. I've thrown up around two pints of blood. He presses my abdomen asking where it hurts. My stomach is killing me. My head's throbbing and I'm totally wiped out. He puts me on a blood transfusion. Doctor and nurses leave. It's hard to find a position where I'm not in pain, on my side is best and I lie there semiconscious, waiting for what will happen next.

I come round gasping for air. I'm lying on my back and there's a gurgling noise in my chest when I try to breathe. The air isn't getting through. My lungs are burning, I'm in agony but I can't move. I simply don't have the energy to even raise my head. Liquid is sloshing about in my lungs. I try to call out but there's no air to power my voice. It feels like I'm drowning.

I've run out of air once before. I was underwater, in the swimming pool, taking my bronze life-saving certificate. I had to retrieve a plastic brick from the bottom of the deep end, fourteen feet down. I was already short of breath from treading water for ten minutes in pyjamas and when I kicked down to find the brick I knew I hadn't enough air in my lungs. But there was no going back so I carried on regardless, too keen to please for my own good.

Down at fourteen feet I looked around and couldn't see the brick. I'm short sighted and didn't have any goggles. By the time I located the brick my lungs were bursting. I picked it up and kicked back to the surface, but not fast enough. I breathed in. When the water hit my lungs it burned like hot tar. I surfaced hacking my guts out but with the brick held triumphantly in my hand. Some lifesaver, I thought.

Now, it's like that time in Kingston Baths, only ten times worse. It's terrifying because I'm *not* underwater in the deep end. Oxygen is all around me but I can't get any. I panic. I'm drowning in air.

I don't think I can hang on but where is there to go? I can't run away. The excruciating pain is everywhere inside me and I'm paralysed. I'm silently screaming swear words. The expletives are nonsense words. I picture them first as monumental letters the size of skyscrapers, then as gigantic letters marching around the curvature of the earth. As each one lands, the earth shudders from the impact. I'm trying to distract myself but it's not working. I search for a place to hide, a box deep inside my head in which to escape the pain. There isn't one.

I try again to call a nurse but no sound comes out. The horrible gurgling noise bubbles in my lungs. I'm losing consciousness; the peripheries of my vision are starting to cloud over. I know its oxygen starvation and unless I can attract someone's attention, nobody's going to come in time.

I have to try and stay conscious, it's not a choice; I'm fighting for my life. I remember a red call button on the wall above my head but I can't see it. With a titanic effort I manage to lift my right arm over my head. My fingers fumble through the rails of the bed-stand. I feel the round plastic of the call button and push it.

Help arrives. A nurse is shouting, "John, John, can you hear me? John, look at me, open your eyes…" I'm groaning involuntarily. They roll me on my side. The liquid sloshes in my lungs. As they roll me over I crunch up into a foetal position, my knees in my face.

They try to disentangle me but I'm locked. My lungs are flooded. I'm out of oxygen. I'm a ball of pain. I know I'm dying. My mind is racing to find solutions, a get-out clause.

I've done my best. I've managed to attract the nurse's attention. I surrender to whatever's going to happen next. It's out of my hands. The stab of a knife blade pierces my heart. The pain overrides all the rest. It's too much. I can do no more to hang on to life. I've lost the fight.

And suddenly, without any thought or intention, from out of the ball of pain, my consciousness, my awareness of myself in my brain, does a backflip. It's involuntary. Some automatic motor drive kicks in. I feel myself rolling backwards down my neck.

There's an uncontrollable surge, like the compressed pressure of a swimmer bursting to the surface from the deep. I explode out through my chest.

The kernel

I rush upwards and stop, suspended just below the ceiling, looking down at myself crunched up on the bed. What's happening? I haven't a clue. It's intense, mystifying and exciting all at once. I've left my body and I don't know how. I freak out. *What the fuck's going on?* I try and take it in.

My mind is crystal clear. I am as clear-headed as before I first collapsed, in fact more so. The daze of the last few days has gone. The confusion has gone. I'm wide-awake. There's a buzzing noise like the white noise of a detuned TV but with tingly high-pitched bells in the mix.

Below me I can see the nurses straightening out my body. They rush around the bed in an organized panic trying to find the space each to do their own job. While I watch I become aware of something I've missed in the shocking jolt of leaving my body behind. The insufferable pain has disappeared. I feel great. I'm hovering six foot above the end of the bed looking towards my head. Being suspended like this doesn't feel as strange as I know it should feel. I think *this is weird*, in a detached sort of way. And I'm no longer freaking out.

The thing is, I recognise what's happening and it's completely normal. I can recall a memory of this happening before, a memory I didn't think I had until a moment ago. I am cocooned in a buzz of electricity as if I'm surrounded by a static charge. No, not surrounded. I *am* a static charge. That's it. I'm a static charge of electricity like a tiny piece of ball lightning.

I'm totally aware of what's going on and what's just happened. I watch my dead body and at first it doesn't bother me. A simile occurs to me out of nowhere. It's like a husk of wheat blown in the wind after the kernel has been threshed out. I feel a powerful sense of gratitude for my deserted body, a strong attachment, and then I'm overwhelmed by a tragic sense of loss. I thank it wholeheartedly for being such a good body, for carrying me around so well. But I'm no longer inside it. It isn't me anymore; it's just a shell. I am the kernel threshed out of the husk.

Looking at my corpse lying on its deathbed is the strangest thing I could ever imagine, but I'm at peace with the idea. I can't argue with it. It's incontrovertible. I'm so happy to be away from the pain and the prison I was in. Happy I got out of my defunct shell before it killed me.

But it *has* killed me.

But I'm still here, so it *hasn't* killed me.

I deliberate this contradiction quiet calmly. If this is what dying is like it's not so bad after all. I chuckle to myself.

A doctor arrives on the scene. I try and call out to the doctor and nurses: "I'm here! Here I am!" But they can't hear me. I don't know how to get their attention. I can see and hear them so why can't they see me? It's no use so I stop trying.

I'm fascinated by how I feel, every sense is heightened – the tingling electric sensations, the hiss of white noise and now something else I notice. I can see every detail in the sharpest focus imaginable. I can't understand it. I'm not wearing my glasses but I can see ten times better than with them on. My perceptions are hyper-real, clearer than normal reality.

I'm not frightened anymore. What was frightening was being locked in a body that couldn't breathe. By comparison this is OK. I feel cool, self-contained; it all feels so natural, like I've been here before.

I glance out of the window and *whoosh*, straightaway find myself moving through the glass into the garden and, *whoosh*, up into the sky. I can see the hospital wing laid out below me, people coming through the public entrance on one side of the wing, the metal bins, gas cylinders and a dumper truck around the back. Traffic passes on the road. The world is carrying on as normal. It's only me that isn't. My aerial perspective is bizarre. As soon as I realise I'm flying I feel a *whoomp* in my gut and I'm terrified of falling. But I don't fall. I think about what's happening and it's obvious: I can't fall; I'm weightless. Gravity has lost its hold. It's just a matter of having the confidence to counter my fear.

I look back at the window I've just exited and without knowing how, whoosh, I'm back in the room on the ward where porters are lifting my body on to a gurney. I'm just getting used to watching my death play out when something new happens.

I rise up into the ceiling, everything starts to cloud over and the physical world around me fades away. The bed, the room, the nurses and doctor, the garden through the window; all the stuff in the world vanishes.

The mist

I'm in a grey mist lit by a faint light. A moment ago I was in the world, now I'm not. This is a completely different space altogether.

What happened?

Where did all the stuff go?

It feels like the space the mist fills is unimaginably huge. There are no boundaries, no walls. I am absorbed. The dim light is diffused with no obvious source. It is fascinating. I wait to see what will happen and when nothing happens I feel anxious. I call out, at first timidly,

"Hello," sounding tiny and ridiculous. Then, trying to put some authority into my voice,

"Hello, is anyone there?" like I know where 'there' is. Then louder as my courage and fear grow in equal proportion, "Hello? Who's there?" As if I suspect a trespasser on my land. But this isn't my land. It's an empty grey mist. And I can hear myself vocalising but I can't tell if my voice is carrying. No one replies.

Fear begins to take hold but I know I can't let it get the better of me. I'm alone. No one is going to come and help if I fuck up. I get a grip on myself. I rationalise. I reckon this has to be some sort of journey and this is only a stop along the way. Except I need to know where I am and where to go next if I'm to deal with the fear building inside me. But there are no directions, no signposts, no horizon, no up or down, no right or left. There is no geography.

Trying to locate myself in this space becomes vital. I can feel my body, my arms and legs, the tingling of limbs. I can sense that I am standing upright, not lying down, but I'm not standing on anything. I'm suspended, weightless in the mist, and it's unnerving. I try not to think about it. Seeing as I can feel my physical presence, I expect to be able to see some sort of shape. But I can't locate myself. When I look down expecting to see the body I can feel, nothing is there. I'm not here anymore. The thought invades my mind. I can see the mist lit by the gloom, but where are my eyes?

A wave of panic overwhelms me. I fight it. I try and suck in oxygen, telling myself to breathe deeply but I'm not breathing anymore. I don't have to and I've only just noticed. I try and calm down. I tell myself, *Look, you're here now, there's nothing you can do about it at the moment. Just hang in there and see what happens.* But it doesn't work. I'm lost.

Waves of anxiety roll through me. The detachment I felt before has long evaporated. I can't see where I am or where to go next. A crushing feeling of loneliness takes hold of me, an empty black hole of aloneness, a physical ache of longing for the world and everything in it. But there's no going back. However much I want to I simply don't know how. I'm dead.

I try and think things through. I know it's too early for me to die – I'm certain of this. I'm not ready, my whole life's ahead of me. I'm just about to leave school, win my freedom and start making my own choices. A life fuelled by television dreams has all come to nothing. I haven't dived the coral reefs like Jacques Cousteau or trekked through the rainforests like David Attenborough. I'll never see the Pyramids or the giant heads of Easter Island. The dunes of the Sahara, the savannahs of the Masai Mara, the icecaps of the Himalayas, the jungles of Borneo are all lost to me. My ambitions will always, forever and ever, remain unfulfilled.

Another regret hits me like a punch to the gut, much stronger than my lost dreams. I'm in love with Jenny Simmons and I haven't told her. She doesn't know. This is suddenly the most important thing. On top of everything else I've lost: my body, my ambitions, my life; this feeling of unrequited love is the most tragic loss I have ever experienced. Everything was to come and now it's gone.

I'm gripped by these thoughts. And another one dawns on me. One I want to push away but takes hold and won't let go. What if this is where you go after you die and nothing else ever happens? What if you hang out alone in this mist forever and that's it? The isolation is a pain tearing me apart from inside out. I wait. Fingers of desperation creep across my mind. And then it comes.

In the Dark

Something's coming my way. I can sense a presence but can't see it. Terror takes hold. Somehow I know this presence is evil. It has smelt my scent and like a hunter it's stalking its prey. It's hunting me. It has my scent. I can feel it approaching, from a great distance, at a frightening speed.

I look frantically left and right, up and down and then I see it rising from below through the mist. Is it rising or am I falling? I don't know which. Have I been falling all this time in the mist and not realised? I don't know that either. But it's too late to figure these things out.

The presence is rushing at me like the ground rushes up at a parachutist. It swallows the dull light and dispels the mist. It's hard to see but as it closes I can make out thrashing limbs and gnashing teeth. A mass of writhing arms entangled together. I can feel it boiling with malice. It's growing bigger. It's filling my world. I know without a shadow of doubt it is evil come to life.

It's here.

I plunge in as if I'm plunging into quicksand. I lose sight of where I am. It's pitch black. The smell is noxious. I gag. Knarled hands grip my legs. Sharp claws tear at my flesh. I can't see my legs, I don't have any but the pain is the same as if they were still there. They have me in their grip as more hands claw for a hold around my thighs, around my waist. Behind the mass of writhing limbs spiteful voices spit abuse.

"We've got you."
"You're ours now."
"There's no escape." They taunt me.
"You're a worthless piece of shit."
"Fresh meat."
"For us to devour."
"A feast. A feast." This becomes a rallying cry as more arrive.
"We gnaw your flesh."
"We eat your heart."

"And you'll never die. You're dead already." They're gleeful. Like screaming harridans.

"We'll devour you for ever and ever," like carping harpies.

"It will never stop."

"We know all about you." And it's true. They can read my thoughts. They're inside my mind.

"You're one of us now. You're too weak to escape."

I feel naked.

"You know you can't beat us." I'm totally exposed.

"You don't even know where you are." They're right. I don't.

"You're worthless, you're good for nothing." And that's how I feel.

"You think you're so important. You're naught." I am nothing.

"You're becoming one of us."

"One of us."

"One of us."

"You're finished." They're scornful.

"We've got you now." And they have.

I could never have imagined such evil and such glee. They're spiteful, vindictive, and victorious. I am their prey. I can't see who is talking – the voices don't reveal themselves. I have the impression they are the voices of masters skulking behind their minions in the blackness out of reach.

I struggle against the gnarly hands gripping my body. The claws scratch, teeth bite. But from somewhere inside me I find strength and I know I'm stronger than they are. Not stronger than the mass but stronger than each in turn. I wrestle, tearing one off as another takes its place. More come to fight. There's so many of them. They're legion.

Somehow, I know their purpose, for just as they can read my thoughts, I can begin to read theirs. And horrified, I realise they are human. Demonic humans perverted and distorted out of all sense of humanity. I can tap into their intentions. They are consumed by malice and spite. Their greatest pleasure is in hurting others.

I understand that their purpose is to catch as many as possible like me who come their way, and to drag them down into this black world where there is no light to see by. I feel icy cold. All good has been perverted into hate.

"Good? What's good, stupid?" They're reading my thoughts.

"There's no good here."

Now I can tell the voices are the masters behind their servants. I fight them with my thoughts. *Goodness is happiness. Goodness is heartfelt. Happiness is strong.* They're thrilled and cackle at my stupidity.

"Good is weak. Hate is strong."

A chorus starts up.

"Good is weak. Hate is strong. Good is weak. Hate is strong."

Mining their nature I can feel the strength of their hatred. They are delighted and excited at their ability to hurt. A corrupting attachment to the power of hate makes them spiteful and malicious, bitter and twisted. I can sense all this as I am sucked into their evil minds.

And as they master my mind I feel the pressure of more crowds fighting for a chance to get their claws into me. The smell of putrid flesh is overpowering and I retch even as I'm thinking how weird, I don't have a nose to smell with. I'm ripping them off, one by one, but there are always more waiting. They have a hold on my body like a python tightening its coils.

"Give up."

"You can't beat us."

"You know it and we know it too."

"You've lost this fight." And somehow I know if I lose this fight it is forever.

I can't tell how long I've been in their clutches. It's impossible to say. Time here isn't like time on earth. It's nebulous in this place. It all happens now, in the present, but simultaneously there's an eternal quality to the passing of each moment. I can feel what it is like to experience this place forever. Both sorts of time are there at once. 'Forever' takes on an ominous meaning. I can feel the crushing weight of eternity and what it will feel like, and I despair.

I lash out; they laugh.

"We've got you now, there's no escape." When I pull one way, their claws anticipate my move. When I try and pull another way, they're there, waiting to reinforce their grip. All this time I'm fighting blind. I can't see my attackers and that's as terrifying as the pain they're inflicting.

A chorus starts chanting,

"Told you so, told you so, told you so, told you so..."

However, probing further into their minds as my own becomes entangled in theirs, I find they are not as secure as they make out. My attackers are driven by a bully's pleasure but also by a victim's fear – a need to be like the rest; one of the gang. I am a temporary distraction from an eternity spent battling it out with each other. When they're through with me they'll attack the weakest of their own kind; each one of them is also a potential target.

The demonic servants are trapped by their masters in the same way they are trying to trap me. They're pathetic. They've chosen to be this way, to join the cohorts of malice. I sense that they've made their choice a long time ago and, behind their bravado, they know it too. Things could have been different for them if only they'd chosen a different course. They can't stand the idea of any beings not being like themselves. I sense they're driven by jealousy. And these thoughts give me the idea there must be others who have escaped their clutches. That this is not the only place I could have fallen into. And that means there must be a different choice if only I knew what it was.

But it's too late. They're winning. They are draining me of energy, sucking it out of me. Many arms are wrapped around my limbs, or more accurately, what were my limbs. Four or five hands claw higher towards my neck. More are rallying to the call. The longer I'm trapped the more beings are grabbing hold. I wrestle them in terror, ripping them off as others find a grip.

I'm getting weaker, losing my strength. They have my neck. They're strangling me. I need to do something to escape right now, immediately, but what am I supposed to do?

It's hopeless and they read my hopelessness. They feed on it. Hopelessness is their meat, their feast. It's what they crave. They laugh at my despair and their success.

I'm almost out of strength, but I'm still fighting out of terror of what will happen when I lose.

"You can fight as much as you like, it won't do you any good." They cackle with glee. They like their victims to fight. Fighting is what they do best.

How to escape? I haven't a clue. These demonic humans have created an evil world out of such darkness in order to exclude any possibility of hope. And I'm getting sucked down further into a future with no escape. It's only a matter of time before they submerge me and make me a creature of the dark just like them. The stench makes me gag. I know they'll have me if they can suffocate me in their grip, so I don't stop struggling, but that simply makes their bonds tighter.

Although I'm in a losing battle the rational part of my mind is still working. Reading their minds as I somehow can, I realise that if these demons hadn't had such an attachment to malice and spite in their human lives, maybe things could have been different for them.

I have an idea. It only takes an instant in this eternity but it's complex. Somehow, I know that this whole experience is energetic: everything in existence is about positive and negative energy. The energy of atoms that repel and attract. The forces that hold the whole universe together: as true for the cosmos as for the universe inside my mind. I tell myself the demons aren't real. They're just a negative manifestation.

"He thinks we're not real." They crow.

"You'll soon know what's real when you join us."

"We are all there is. There is nothing else."

"Join us. You have no choice. You've already lost the fight." They pull harder, downwards. As I tear them off it's getting difficult to focus but I stick with my idea. If this evil is energetic then what I need to do is to call on positive energy to give me strength, to enlist forces for good. To do something in death I've learnt not to do in life. I need to ask for help.

I can't call on any Christian god and suddenly find allegiance for a religion I've never believed in. Neither does it feel right to call upon Buddha, Buddhism being the closest religion that makes any sense to me. I'm not a Buddhist. This is no time for an insincere conversion. Any pretence will backfire on me. The battle I'm waging depends on the utmost integrity, complete honesty about myself. I can't fake it – the demonic humans will know. I'm battling for my consciousness: whether I'll remain independent or be sucked into the dark.

I know that this can't be all there is in the universe. Not everything is so evil. From the deepest, most honest place inside me, deeply rooted in my core, I find a sense of wonder at the beauty of creation. Sunrise through early morning mists, wind rustling through oak woods, the crash of waves on sandy beaches, the arc of the horizon from the top of a mountain. And all the creatures that live in creation: the iridescence on a butterfly's wings, the waving arms of sea anemones in a rock pool. I focus on the impossible beauty of a leaf, the majesty of a tree, my amazement at the existence of everything from insects to elephants. I know that creation isn't evil. I cry out for help from the places where the animals roam, from all the forces for good in the universe.

But it doesn't sound right. Who am I calling out to? I try again.

"To all the Forces in Nature. To the Wonder of Creation. To All that is Good." And I add how I feel.

"I know I'm nothing to you but please help me, I can't fight any longer. I need your help. Help me. Now." I repeat my incantation, rephrasing it as I think of more ways to frame my appeal.

"To all that's Good in the World, to the Beauty of Life, to the Wonders of Nature..." No help arrives. And why should it? As I cry out for help, what's left of my strength disappears. I'm consumed by the demons, swallowed into their pitch-black world of hate, and in my final moments of freedom I appreciate the tiny insignificance of my infinitesimal existence.

*

Something happens. Something is grabbing me from behind, from under my armpits, if I still had any, and starts to pull me up, away from the clawing hands. My spirits start to lift, I can't tell what's happening but a spark of hope ignites inside me, followed by joy. I feel energised. My strength's returning. The demons are losing their grip. They snarl. They thrash about trying to get hold of me.

I turn round to look for my rescuer and see an oily black void as vast as outer space and in the void towering over me there's an ephemeral translucent radiance of light. It's utterly beautiful, like a cirrus cloud made of strands of light that sparkle. Tiny stars are exploding inside the strands. It moves by itself as if light can be thick and heavy and slow. Somehow I know the light is masculine.

I look back. In the light from this being I can see a vast field of clawing limbs extending as far as the glow from my rescuer. Faces and bodies are obscured underneath outstretched arms and I can't see their masters either in the gloom, but the sheer scale is horrifying.

As I'm lifted to safety my confidence begins to return. I'm happy to be alive. The absurdity of that thought makes me laugh and laughter fuels my happiness. The demonic humans hate my laughter and this makes me laugh even more. I'm laughing with heartfelt joy and that's precisely what they can't stand. It's acid to them. They shriek and screech and set about attacking each other. I rise upwards faster and faster. I can still see them thrashing about below me, receding into the distance.

A physical sensation of thoughts passes through me. It's not a voice, it's more than a voice; it's an emotional understanding. The thoughts come from the strands of light.

He tells me he's here to help. He's a guardian and he is my guide.

I'm overcome with gratitude.

Another thought wave explains there is no need for gratitude. This is his purpose.

Happiness floods through me. I feel like a heroic explorer and I'm looking forward to what might happen next.

*

I'm travelling super fast through the oily black void, my guide at my side. There is no wind rushing in my hair, no g-force compressing my etheric body, but I know we are somehow moving on and on. I have so many questions but I sense they're all too trivial to ask. I'm trying to analyse what's happening, as if I were still alive and science could answer all my questions. But this is outside of any science I know. The fact I'm here at all is already impossible to comprehend. I'm also in awe of the power that envelops me. I'm anxious that if I start asking stupid questions he'll realise he's made a mistake and drop me back into the world of the demons.

From out of the black void, above and off to the right, a tiny speck of light appears. If my sense of geography is correct it is so far in the distance it must be hundreds of miles away. My guide informs me it is my destination.

The tiny light is a pinprick in the vast emptiness of space. I move towards the light. I don't know how I'm doing this with no arms or legs, no physical shape at all, but it feels natural. I'm flying faster and faster, accelerating at a phenomenal speed. Of course, for all I know I could be at a standstill, motionless in the void. The light could be rushing towards me in the same way it felt like the malevolent demons rushed towards me like predators closing in on their prey. But I know without questioning it's the other way round. The light is there in the distance and I'm flying towards it.

At least it feels like I'm flying but on reflection, and I have an eon to reflect, a better comparison would be floating. As if I'm suspended underwater in a crystal clear sea and I am caught in a current, streaming towards the light. It's effortless and I feel no wind or g-force because I'm moving at the same speed as the current.

I realise my guardian, my guide has disappeared. Fixated on the pinprick of light and my own thoughts, I didn't feel him go. One moment we were together and the next, I'm alone again. But it's OK. I'm not freaking out. I know he has set me on the right course.

*

As I rush towards the light, a screen appears in my way. I crash into the screen and fleetingly find myself inside a scene from my life. It's like a snippet of a film shot from my point of view. No sooner have I recognised the memory that I burst out the other side of the screen and another is rushing towards me. I crash through that one and another memory is contained inside.

I smash though one screen after another, momentarily reliving scenes from my life as if watching a disjointed movie. Except it's a fully immersive experience in 3D, in which I not only see and hear but also feel the emotions I felt at the time.

I watch my life unravel. Hundreds of remembered moments speed by. Whoosh, whoosh, the scenes pass through me as other screens appear. Each event is locked into the location where it happened: little pockets of time and space. There is no apparent significance to the memories that appear, it's all happening so fast. Whoosh,

whoosh, scene by scene, moments from my life replay and I relive them, the circumstances, the places, the people.

Kew Gardens' hot houses, giant golden carp swimming languidly in a lily-covered pool, whoosh, an archaeological dig in a trench, the thrill of uncovering a Roman amulet, whoosh. And I grasp that there's logic at play. I'm travelling backwards. The screens started in the present and as my life rewinds I'm getting younger and younger from adolescence back into childhood.

Running through woods outside Washington DC, whoosh, at the top of the Empire State Building, whoosh, climbing down a flooded cave with my father and sister without ropes or hardhats. It feels like many more memories are passing through me than I can see on the screens, too fast for me to catch. A classroom in junior school, year seven, Mr Alexander calls me to the front for doodling and then admires my picture, whoosh. Auntie Mabel, full of Christmas cheer, embraces me in a bear hug, whoosh.

All these memories resonate emotionally. Now I'm seven, in the sea at Littlehampton, I fall off a groyn, slash my leg, whoosh, I'm five, in the school playground, whoosh, and then I'm three, my mother is screaming at me, she won't stop, whoosh, then two, at my grandparents, and then the screens disappear. I've run out of memories. The final curtain has closed on the movie of my life and I'm back in the black void being drawn towards the light at a fantastic speed.

A name is all that's left of my identity. I am John. But there is no John anymore. He's dead and I recognise intuitively that I have to give him up. Only I don't want to. I resist. My name is all I have left. What is there apart from this tiny attachment to my sense of self? But it's clear that my name is a construction, an artifice. My identity, seventeen years of accumulated self, layer on layer like an onion, is not important anymore. In fact, it's an obstacle. So I give up my name, my self, I am no longer John, I am…

I am here, I remain. I don't know who or what I am anymore but I feel liberated, unencumbered alone in the infinite black void. And with these new feelings comes more knowledge. I know intuitively that I have become myself, the thing I was before I became John. I have no shape or size, I can't define myself but I feel courageous in this infinity.

The closer I get to the light the bigger it becomes. Now it is a rectangle, longer in height than width. It looks like a doorway. The light inside the doorway is dazzling white, the light of a thousand suns but it doesn't blind me and it has a strange quality. However bright it is, no light spills out into the void. It shines but it doesn't radiate. It's contained.

As I approach the doorway it is much bigger than I first thought. It's the size of a planet and I can't see to its edges. I'm crossing into the light, entering through the doorway, but it's impossible to say exactly where the border lies. I can only see one edge of the doorway as I pass. The border between the light and the dark void isn't solid like a doorframe, it swirls like smoke in still air. It is made of a myriad of lights all clumped together like a forest of thousands of fibre optic lights.

Everything is so extreme I should be mortified beyond any fear on earth but I'm not. From the moment my guide rescued me I've been in a state of wonder – excited, nervous, curious – but fear has disappeared.

As I cross the border I am embraced by a stream of new feelings; emotions that emanate from the light. A massive waterfall of love cascades through me. Love of a quality and intensity I've never felt before. It's not like some versions of love I've experienced in life: selfish, conditional, obsessive. It is real, unselfish, unconditional and compassionate. It's all-encompassing and surges through me like a tropical storm. I am ecstatic. I soak it up. And in this embracing love something else dawns on me. It's an immutable truth I've always known but momentarily, in life, I've forgotten.

I've been here before. I feel the joy of returning home.

I am so happy. I'm so astonished. I shout,

"I'm home. I've come home."

And I know it's true.

In the Light

The overwhelming love feeds my self-confidence. Without it I'd be totally freaked, terrified out of my wits. The sense of my own insignificance inside this vast measureless space is daunting. As it is, I surf on the love. I want to stay like this forever.

Inside the gigantic doorway, shapes start to appear. A landscape of clouds, the most beautiful cumulonimbus I've ever seen. More real, somehow more solid, than any clouds I've ever seen on earth. Every detail is crystal sharp, etched in the clean white light. The fact I can see things without having eyes no longer strikes me as bizarre. My visual perception is unlike anything I've experienced either awake or in a dream. It has an unimaginable clarity, a knifelike sharpness.

The clouds tower above and sink below me as far as I can see. There is a vast canyon between two banks of cloud and I fly through it. As I look around I focus on one outcrop. Whoosh. Suddenly I've jumped there. It's instantaneous. I move my focus to another cloud and whoosh, jump there too. To focus my attention is to travel. It's a complete surprise. I've discovered how to move and I'm thrilled. I had expected simply to be taken where the current flows but now I can jump from one place to the next just by looking and intending. I focus on another cloud far away and flit, I'm there. I haven't a clue what's going to happen next, but now I can control where I'm going I feel like a pilot in my own cockpit.

One of the most extraordinary things in this extraordinary world is that none of this feels strange to me. There's just a deep, joyful recollection of a familiar landscape. Although each new discovery is a surprise, it's not as if I'm discovering how to exist here for the first time. It's more like I'm rediscovering things I've forgotten.

And I haven't forgotten where I come from either. I remember Kingston, Kew, parents, friends and how it felt to be alive. But all the things I thought were the most important, like who I was, what I was doing or my place in the world, are now insignificant. Along with the less important things like my most cherished possessions, collections of fossils, posters, records, guitars, songs I'd composed, pictures I'd painted. These were simply the things I had accumulated to define John. I can look back on that life from the perspective of this new one. It hasn't gone away but it's only a shadow compared to this. I laugh at how seriously life takes itself and how long it seems to last, when from this new perspective the whole of life on earth is just a momentary blip in time.

I approach the outer reaches of one of the clouds. I'm getting closer and closer and I can see shapes inside it: myriads of separate lights, each light encased inside an egg-like globe of jelly matter. I gaze into one of them. The light inside only shines within its jelly-like package. At its centre, the light is pure white and tails off towards the casing. I can make out shapes and details. There are complex patterns of veins, dark and light, coming from the centre and radiating outwards to the shell. It's captivating. I try to judge the size of one of these eggs but I have no comparison, I don't even know my own size.

Through the translucent parts of the first wall of globes I can see others behind, and more behind those. I don't know about the rest, but this cloud is actually made of these light eggs. Millions, no, billions of them tightly compressed together. It's amazing. And I know straightaway that each one of these lights is conscious as surely you would know that a stranger on a street is human. Every light is contained in its own translucent package and each one is aware. They are beautiful.

Information ripples between the light globes like waves of energy. I can sense their energy and their thoughts, though I cannot read them. Drifting in the current of absolute love, I get the feeling they are waiting, but for what?

Another question crosses my mind: if these lights are globes of consciousness, then what am I? I must be a light globe too. How could I be different? That would make me unique, and I finished being unique when I relinquished my identity. I'm just a single source of light, one of billions, drifting in the space between the clouds.

A banal comparison occurs to me. The light globes look like frogspawn but seen in negative; the black dot at the centre of each egg is white, not black, and the surrounding egg sac darker, not lighter. They're all clumped together in a stream. All of these 'eggs' and me are feeding on the energy blasting through us like frogspawn washed by an oxygen-rich river current. I want to find out where the current's coming from.

The Light Beings

A string of lights peels off from the cloud I'm closest to. There are maybe a dozen although I don't count them. They form a circle on one level plane with me in the centre. I'm surrounded. I could escape but there's no indication that anything bad is going to happen. One of the lights rushes to my side and starts to communicate in the same remarkable way as the guardian who rescued me from the dark. In shared understandings. And I reply using the same thought transference. It's so intuitive it's as if I've always had this ability.

The light is an old friend I have forgotten completely, coming to renew our friendship. Although I have forgotten my friend in life we have known each other here for eternity. He or she (there is no gender in this place) is ecstatic to see me again because there is something heroic in what I have done, to have lived and died in a human life, though I haven't a clue what it is. I'm simply thrilled to meet again.

The circle of lights communicates with me, sometimes all together, sometimes in turn. The light emanating from them increases when they 'speak'. Each is a being, a wise and compassionate being of light. They share the same consciousness and simultaneously exist as individuals. Our 'conversation' is in concepts. Compressed bubbles of thought: compacted information and emotions, each 'bubble' containing questions and answers to whatever is in my thoughts or whatever is in theirs.

The quality of knowledge they communicate is very different from what we think of as knowledge on earth. In life we arrive at what we call knowledge through observation, reasoning, argument, and debate; or else, with blinkered-vision, selfish motives, by force of will and ignorance. Our emotions govern what we choose to know. The knowledge the Light Beings impart is more certain than any force of will, intellectual hypothesis or scientific proof. It's more certain than faith because faith needs belief, and this knowledge doesn't depend on belief.

Each answer contains all the descriptions of every different angle and every possible solution, and each has a compassionate understanding for the inevitable conflicts and resolutions that come to play in each question. The place where every answer ends is a place where all the strands bind together into a whole. I am being presented with universal wisdom that simply is.

This is this.

That is that.

Everything makes such beautiful and perfect sense, it is blissful.

And with the joy of understanding comes a sense of humour. I suggest some ironic insight to one of their answers and the Light Beings chuckle and share one themselves in return; a much funnier and far deeper observation. Profound understandings inevitably lead to laughter at the absurdity of life, the beauty of existence, the wonderful construction of the cosmos. We share jokes, although these jokes are about the most insightful truths.

Some answers are illustrated visually. A plane of liquid appears on the same plane as the circle of Light Beings and myself. An answer drops into the plane of liquid like a pebble dropped into a still pond and concentric rings of information ripple from the centre outwards, right through me and into infinity. I experience the answers physically. As each ripple expands inside my consciousness I expand too. The Light Beings are immersing every fibre of my being in knowledge.

However, as I grasp each answer and try to hold on to it there's a problem. My attention can't focus on all the ripples at once. The sheer amount of information being transmitted is too much. Each thought bubble is as solid as an iceberg but as I absorb the whole structure in all its fantastic complexity, the iceberg splinters and melts back into the sea.

"Where am I?" I ask.

Where I am is the source of everything, a dimension of light where all life in all its myriad of forms is made and where it returns to be remade according to its nature. It is the place of all knowledge, all pasts and all futures, where everything can be seen at once and nothing is hidden.

There is more, much more. But I can't possibly take in the full breadth and depth of what the voices are revealing. I'm taken wherever the answer takes me. Waves of understanding wash over me and then they're gone, past recall. The answer concludes with the reassurance, "This is the universe of Light and the Light is Home." I feel it, the sense of completeness, of belonging, the rightness of it and the sense of return.

I am Home.

I frame another question. "Who was I?"

The Light Beings show me my life. Shimmering screens appear like the projector screens I burst through on the way to the Light. But I don't burst through these screens. The Light Beings are tapping into moments from my life and I watch myself interacting with people I knew. The images are like a film but three-dimensional. I can step in and out of the scenes and change my position within them.

Before, on the way to the Light, I saw everything from my own point of view. Now I can see everything from the perspective of other people and what effect I had on them. I feel their emotions as if they are my own. The Light Beings are not recreating these scenes, they are actually replaying them, as if there is a library where all these memories are stored; to be relived at will.

They show me what I achieved, however little in a life so short. They congratulate me for my successes but these aren't what I'd always thought they were: not passing exams or winning swimming galas; the things I'd never thought about are the most crucial. Every example of understanding, honesty and empathy counts more here than any so-called achievement back on earth. Little acts of kindness, acts of compassion. Taking the time to listen and to give advice. Things I'd done to help others without thinking twice about it.

Next I ask, "Who were the demonic humans?"

And the Light Beings answer. And I understand. It was as I thought when I was in their grip. They are those who become lost through their own choices in life. The Light Beings don't want to dwell on this subject. They find it distasteful. It bears little importance to them. As for me, I am no longer my old self, the one who was trapped by the demonic humans, and surfing in the current of love it no longer matters to me either.

Another thought. I ask, "So who am I now?"

And again before I have even framed the question an encyclopaedic answer has exploded in my consciousness. "You are a being of potential the same as the other beings of light you encountered in the clouds. You are drawn to this cosmos. You will travel to your place in this cosmos or you will return, or you will progress. These are your possibilities."

"What are the clouds of light globes doing?"

"They are waiting," and I am shown a stream of globes peeling off from the clouds and cascading into the black void like the spray of water droplets in a vast waterfall. The globes of light are returning to the mortal physical world.

I am so astoundingly happy to be here I never want to leave, so I ask, "Why are they going back?"

In the answer there is a deep and melancholic longing for the feelings of flesh, touch and taste, sight and smell, weight and gravity. A forgetfulness of what it is like to inhabit the physical world. A deep-seated ennui, the feeling that the light globes have already waited for a great length of time in the clouds of light. I also detect their desire to right wrongs, correct previous mistakes, and an ultimate goal: to evolve into a higher being. A wish that is understood to be possible only by returning to the physical world for another lifecycle.

"We are all beings of light. We manifest in the physical world in individual ways, with or without any particular awareness of our manifestation. That world believes in itself, not in us. In that world we exist as detached, separate individuals. As you can see, this is an illusion. We are all joined together and to the Source."

"What is the Source?"

The Light Beings show me. In an instant we have jumped location. The light, previously the radiant yellows and oranges of sunsets, changes to copper and gold. We approach a wall of cloud obstructing our flight, and just as I think we're about to collide, a canyon appears and we fly through.

We are there.

The Source is the size of a planet. It looks like the folded petals of a beautiful semi-tropical flower, like a protea flower head. Everything is made of radiant golden light but the light is solid. The flower head is like the mouth of a volcano. The petals slowly pulse open and closed and a river of golden liquid like molten lava pores out through the petals and flows all around us. Its power is overwhelming. An intense rush of wind from the Source is as hot as a blast furnace. One of the Light Beings transmits an understanding: The lava is the river of life and the blast of energy I'm feeling is the breath of the Source. It creates the current I've been swimming in. The golden river of life flows out of this world into our world energetically, in the same way that solar winds blast the earth. But this isn't like nuclear fission inside the Sun. The Source is the universal generator of worlds. The all-seeing, all-knowing Creative Force. The Source isn't like the Light Beings or myself – its intelligence is not like ours at all. It is One. The intensity is frightening. I sense I'd be crushed like a knat if it weren't for my companions.

The Light Beings have shown me all that I can handle and we jump back to the canyon of clouds where we started. After my encounter I have so many questions. I ask about the reasons for life, the point of it all, and the reply – an answer that contains all answers simultaneously – is simple:

"Love and wisdom. Wisdom and love. The search for one leads to the other; two routes to the same destination. They are one and the same. The highest creative achievement in existence."

And this is palpable here in the light that is full of both absolute wisdom and unconditional love, but I can see that on Earth the answer would seem incomplete. I hadn't phrased the question correctly in my mind. My question is more about meaning.

"But *why* are we here? What is the purpose of existence?"

Questioning their previous answer makes me feel like a precocious child but the Light Beings enjoy my persistence. They answer and my mind tries to grasp it, but as the first wave of ripples washes through me, another follows and another, expanding and expanding faster than previous answers, faster than I can follow and without holding on to the meaning of the first wave I'll never get to see the full picture and… I've lost it. Too much information.

The little I manage to hold on to is this: "We are the eyes and ears of the Universe," but without the rest it makes little sense. I reckon the Light Beings knew that already, because they're chuckling to themselves.

*

I stop asking questions. The last answer was too much for me and now the Light Beings have their own agenda. There are more things they want me to see.

We fly through another canyon and I'm astounded to see a magnificent city of light supported on the cliff faces of the clouds. I laugh in amazement. It glints and shimmers. It sparkles like quartz. The whole city is crystalline, built in many styles from different ages. It reminds me of pictures of Petra, the Parthenon, Hagia Sofia, Mont St Michel, Luxor, Angkor Wat and Chartres. Architectural styles are seamlessly interwoven. We close in and float past the crystal city. I'm speechless marvelling at the detail and intricate design. A latticework of finely wrought colonnades sits, one on top of the next, climbing the face of a valley with streets, passages and staircases snaking in and out of each building's façade.

We jump scene several times. Into a factory full of machines like old printing presses from the time of Gutenberg but made of light. Into a sort of textile mill, weaving materials from threads of light. Into a square inhabited by amorphous people; no longer light globes but shaped like humans and engaged in some sort of work I don't understand.

The city recedes into the distance as we fly back through the clouds. Further and further back. From this new perspective the Light Beings show me how their universe appears to them. It's an infinitely complex matrix of lights, fantastical in scale. Each cluster of lights is its own galaxy and all are connected to each other. I'm laughing with astonishment and joy at the panorama laid out in front of me.

But the Light Beings interrupt my reverie. They are communicating a concept I don't want to hear. I get as angry as a child throwing a tantrum. The concept is:

"This is not your time. Your time has yet to come. You are to return to your world."

I don't want to go back. I never want to go back. I've gone through so much pain to get here; death, the grey mist, the demons in the Dark. I am Home. I fight against the idea but I know I have no choice.

The Light Beings communicate more advice. A plane of liquid appears similar to the others but with a different purpose. This is the lake of human potential. It surrounds us and contains every human emotion – from anger to sadness, fear to hope, wonder to despair, love to hate. Each emotion is a facet of personality that manifests as a ripple in the lake. I am in the middle and I can experience each facet as if each one is available to choose.

The placid surface distorts into waves, stretching to accommodate my choices. They form peaks and troughs and then collapse as I move on. By comparison with the love in which I've been floating, many of the feelings are unpleasant, clearly representing bad choices. Experiencing all the different potentials in this way leaves me with only one choice as to the personality that best suits me. And when I've made my choice the lake calms.

The Light Beings tell me that the configuration I've chosen is already my own character. This wasn't an exercise in choice, as I'd thought, it was an illustration of the potential I'd already chosen. They advise me about my potential, how it is mine alone, how everyone has their own potential and how, although we interact with each other to fulfil our potentials, each of us is on our own unique journey.

They warn me about the possible consequences of my potential. Warnings about those who will seek to take advantage, to manipulate and control me for their own ends that I don't want to hear and choose to ignore. Cocooned in the absolute happiness of being here I feel strong enough to take anything that's thrown at me. I am invincible. I accept my potential unquestioningly.

There is a final lesson in the lake of human potential that the Light Beings want me to learn.

"Only through the mind can the world be seen. Only through the heart can it be understood. Perception is in the mind. Love is in the heart. Life is an opportunity to learn. Try and use the opportunity as we have shown you. It's your potential to use it well."

As I'm fighting the idea that I'm going to have to go back, a thought crosses my mind, something that might make up for losing all of this.

"Won't it be amazing to tell people about this place and what I've seen?"

And in the thought the answer happens.

"If you try and tell people about this place, they won't believe you. The world only sees itself. Only a few can see past the illusion of matter. We are beyond that world. Only a few can remember where they come from."

The answer comes with the idea that even though they've answered everything I've asked, there will be a limit to what I will be able to remember. This restriction comes with a perfect explanation of why this will happen, which I also won't be able to remember. Something to do with free will, I don't know what.

The circle of Light Beings tells me my journey isn't quite over. I can travel forwards, further into the clouds before I have to return. My superior companions bid me farewell, and with heartfelt thanks and regret at leaving such wise advisors and loving friends, I float into the clouds. I feel a great excitement. What's out there? Where am I going? I sense other worlds beyond, other dimensions entirely different from this one. I'm electrified with the prospect of what's ahead. Once again I feel like an intrepid explorer.

But there's something pulling on me. I'm trying to swim forwards but it has taken hold. It feels like a stretched elastic band attached to the base of my spine, my fulcrum, where the spine connects to the hips, but it can't actually be that. I have no form. I struggle against it but I have no leverage. There's nothing to grab on to. The elastic band is stretched to breaking point. I can't go any further.

With a frightening rush I am catapulted backwards through the clouds, back through the doorway of light, back through the black void.

I am overwhelmed with the pain of loss. The world of Light, full of love and wisdom, vanishes. My home has disappeared. I ache with longing. Everything goes black and I lose consciousness.

Return

I wake up and wait a moment before opening my eyes. I can feel myself back inside my body, the enormous weight and pressure of bones and muscle compared to a moment ago. I'm breathing again and after not having had to breathe for what seems like an eternity, it's really hard work. How can people do this all the time?

I open my eyes. My father is sitting upright in a chair against the wall at the foot of the bed staring at his hands. I shift my head slightly on the pillows to see him better. He looks ashen and I want to reassure him.

"Dad, I'm back," I announce.

His face lights up in a broad smile, "John, are you alright?"

I know what he is thinking. It isn't about whether I'm alive – plainly the doctors had resuscitated me – he's worried his son is brain damaged. I sense all this without him saying a word.

"It's alright Dad, I'm back. I'm not a vegetable."

"Oh John it's so good to hear you say that."

I have to tell him what happened. "Dad. I died."

"No you didn't. They resuscitated you."

"No, I mean it. I died. I came out of my body and went…" despite the wrench of the elastic band that pulled me back, it's all there. The memories of where I've just come from are physically tangible; the whole experience in all its mind-bogglingly wonderful metaphysical complexity. I don't know where to start, "…I went to unbelievable places. It was amazing, I can't explain…"

He purses his lips and frowns, "That's alright son. You just rest."

I'm exhausted. Breathing is such a physical effort. Seeing a drip attached to my arm I ask, "What's this for?"

"They're giving you compacted blood cells. You lost a lot of blood and they're putting it back." It makes sense.

"How long was I out?"

"You've been asleep for almost an hour since they brought you back from Intensive Care." Dad gets up, stands by the bedside.

I don't remember Intensive Care. The last thing I remember, in this world, is watching from above as the porters lifted me on to a gurney. I look up at him and try again.

"Dad... I died."

"Your heart stopped," he says, "But you're going to be alright. Rest now."

The afternoon is still sunny. The room is just the same as before. It's only me who has changed. I stare at the beautiful garden through the open window. It's radiant. The colours of the flowers sing, the greens of the plants vibrate, golden shafts of light stream through the window. The sky is bluer than before, the air richer, loaded with fragrance. I'm welling up at the extraordinary beauty of it all, my senses feel as if they're still amplified like they were in the Light.

I say something neither of us has ever said before in our father-son relationship – my stoic northern Dad and his soft southern son – "I love you, Dad."

Even though his son's just returned from the dead he can't say he loves me back. In some intangible way I know that, for him, opening up and saying the word threatens his sense of manliness. "You too, son," he replies. I figure that will do and fall back to sleep.

*

I wake up in the evening of the same day. My mother has been and gone, there are grapes and a get-well card and Dad is no longer there. Through the window the sun is falling out of the sky, pulsing as if it's alive. I'm alone, gazing at the ball of fire until nurses arrive to change the IV, check my pulse and write up my notes. They seem very pleased with me. I wonder why and realise they're pleased I'm here, alive. They've bought me back from the dead. I must have been in a right state.

I recall everything that happened. The memories are crystal clear, the joy, the peace, how it felt to be Home. I try and remember all the lessons I learnt from the Light Beings. I want to cling on to the experience, keep it real.

It changes everything. Life after death is a fact. We exist as astral beings of light. Everything here is made there, in light. There's an energetic source to everything, and it's full of love and wisdom. We are all joined together in a planetary matrix. We are created in the Light and come here to… to do what? It's fuzzy. I can't remember. I try concentrating but it's not something that concentrating can bring back. If anything, thinking about it intellectually only pushes it further away. It was sensory, physical. The telepathic conversations inhabited my whole being. I was a bubble of thought expanding with each lesson and now I can't remember the most important one.

And then there's Jenny. I'm even more in love with Jenny than before all this happened. She was my last attachment to this world. That's how important she is to me. I'm so full of love for Jenny, for the world, for everything, it feels like I'm going to explode. I'm convinced all I have to do is to tell her I love her and she'll tell me she feels the same.

*

The night shift arrives. For the last few hours I've been gazing at the sky as it turns from tangerine to deep inky blue, finally disappearing into black, trying to get my head around everything that's just happened. There is undeniable evidence of where I am right now: the weight of my flesh and bone, the need to inhale, the way the hospital room is constructed, the sun having set; all these things are rooted in the physical world. However, there isn't a doubt in my mind that where I've just been is far more real than here. Even though nothing there had the physical solidity of this world and time behaved in strange ways – present and eternal all at once – it was still a far greater reality than this one.

Everything in the room is just as real as it was when I died and now, compared to those constructions made from light in the clouds, everything is more solid than before – actually a bed, actually a chair. But I can't help questioning their existence. It feels like I've been in the other world for so long that I'm an alien seeing these things for the first time. What is this chair? What is this bed? I know their purpose but I'm having trouble piecing together their nature and why and how they function. The hospital ward, walls, floor and ceiling are more concrete than they were before: heavier, unyielding but somehow more open to questioning. All this stuff just vanished like in the puff of smoke of a magician's disappearing trick. The ceiling turned to mist. Nothing is as solid as it appears. I find myself trying to fit the two worlds together as I know for sure there must be a relationship between here and there. I'm proof of that.

I try and deconstruct the chair by the side of my bed. Is this really made of light or is it what it appears to be: dead metal? Is this a world of matter and the other one a world of energy? How do the two worlds link up, where are the joins? I attempt to trace the route I took. I desperately need to find the geography. Through the window the moon rises, a giant rock hanging weightless in the sky.

This has been the longest day of my life. This morning was literally a lifetime ago and it feels like tomorrow will be the start of a new life altogether, though what exactly makes it new, I haven't a clue. The events of the day are overwhelming. This first night I'm still so close to the Light that not a thought of the bad stuff I experienced crosses my mind. That will come later. For now the world of Light is all there is. The physical sensations are still with me: the weightlessness, the flying, how it felt to be a globe of light.

Along with how it looked: the vast infinity, the clouds, the Source, the city of light.

And how it felt: the love, the wisdom and the absolute certainty of true knowledge that the Light Beings possessed. I lie in my bed feeling blissfully happy and then I remember where I am, back on the surface of this planet, and the loss of that wonderful place hits me again like a punch in the gut. The longing for that other world is physical. It plummets me into an abyss. I've lost Home and I've got a lifetime to wait to get it back.

*

"Morning John. Will you be having some breakfast today?" The catering nurse gives me a menu. I'm ravenous and order everything on it. Cereals, full English breakfast, tea, toast and marmalade. Another nurse arrives and helps me out of bed, careful not to pull the IV out of my arm. She gives me a bottle to pee in and washes me with a flannel as I lean against the bed. Other nurses are scurrying around changing the sheets. I feel faint standing up. Breakfast arrives. Cornflakes and tea is all I'm allowed. This isn't going to fill me up.

The garden through the open window is shrouded in mist. It has an otherworldly appearance. The trees are ethereal shapes hanging in space. As the first rays of the sun penetrate the mist, morning dew sparkles on the flowers. There's a crisp chill dampness to the air. Scents waft into my room. Everything is beautiful.

After breakfast a young doctor arrives. He looks pleased – the same as the nurses the day before. He tells me I happened to be on his shift yesterday. I figure he helped save my life.

"You lost a lot of blood. We suspect an ulcer, somewhere in your stomach or duodenum, we want to do some tests to find out, OK?"

"OK. How much blood did I lose?"

"About eight pints."

That didn't make sense.

"But I only have eight pints don't I?"

"Well it varies. Eight pints is the average but a fit young man like you, six foot tall, you can have as much as ten or eleven pints."

"Eleven?"

"Yes, eleven."

"So I had what? Three pints left?"

"Yes, that'd be about right."

"How did I lose it?"

"We think through your stomach lining. Have your stools been dark recently?"

"Yes... is that how I was losing blood?"

"Yes, that's why you didn't realise."

"And what happened to me?"

"You suffered a cardiac arrest."

"My heart stopped."

"Yes, I'm afraid so."

"It felt like I was drowning. I couldn't breathe, there was liquid in my lungs, I couldn't get any air."

The doctor looks uncomfortable.

"Yes." He says, "You had a Pulmonary Edema." He deliberates, searching for a non-medical explanation. "You're heart hadn't got enough blood to pump round your body. We tried to replace the blood you'd lost to stabilise your system but we did it too fast. Given the stress that your heart was under it started pumping liquid into your lungs."

"So I drowned?"

He stops to think about this.

"Well, yes, you could say that. The flooding in your lungs caused the cardiac arrest. Yes."

"How long was I out for?"

"Your heart stopped for nine minutes."

"Nine minutes?" I'm astonished.

"Well, at least nine minutes. You were in theatre for around nine minutes before we got your heart started again but before that we couldn't apply CPR because of the liquid in your lungs. We're using concentrated red blood cells to try and get your strength back."

As old as I am I've never talked to a doctor one-to-one. I feel grown-up, taking control of my own condition. It's so much easier and more straightforward without my mother around to take control.

"Thanks for explaining what happened to me."

He smiles, "Don't worry, you're going to be alright now, you're in safe hands. We're going to keep you in for a week or two while you fully recover and we run some tests, find out what caused it."

All through our conversation I'm itching to tell him what actually happened to me but I keep my mouth shut. He's a doctor. I reckon from his clinical point of view he'd think I was brain damaged or deranged and want to send me for psychiatric tests on top of all the other tests.

And I remember the advice the Light Beings gave me not to try and describe where I went. I work through the sequence of events. Nine minutes in the theatre. But how long did it take to get me to intensive care? My last recollection was from this room, not the theatre, so I must have been dead for longer than nine minutes. My understanding of medical matters is vague but I'm pretty sure that after a couple of minutes without oxygen, brain damage sets in. Why am I not brain damaged? I don't feel damaged and rattle through as many facts from my A-level revision I can think of to see if anything is missing. It's all there. I think about the timeframe. There isn't enough time to account for my experiences. But time operated by different rules in the other world. Present and eternal.

I retrace my steps over the last few days, wondering how I was still standing with only three pints of blood left in me. I can't have been walking around on only three pints. I'd vomited, say, two pints in the hospital after wrenching my stomach on the banisters as my mother tried to get us to hospital faster than an ambulance. And I must have lost some over the weekend as I got weaker and weaker. Back when I caught the bus I'd probably been running on seven pints, not three.

No wonder my heart was beating double-speed. I remember the pain of being locked in a body that couldn't breathe. It was terrifying. But I'm also looking at it from a different perspective now. I've a sense of detachment, as if the person who went through all that wasn't me. The consciousness in the Light was me. So who am I now? Am I John again, the character I had to let go on the way to the Light? I suppose I am if I'm here. I'm back inside my physical body. I don't feel separate, but I don't feel like myself either.

I want to get out of bed but I'm wiped out. Physically, I don't feel at all joined up. I feel centre-less, like I'm still somewhere else and haven't caught up with myself. I reach out my right hand, touch my left arm and feel my skin. It feels new, like I'm touching it for the first time. I cross my arms and hug my chest. I run my hands over my body, I'm a stranger to my own flesh. It's me but also not me. I don't belong in this body.

A lump forms in my throat. I well up. It's incredible to be back, but looking around the hospital room it feels unreal. I know it's as solid and physical as ever it was, but I don't belong here. I belong in the Light. I close my eyes and reconnect with the sensations I felt there. It's so real, so present. It's like I should be able to reach out and touch it. But I can't.

Along with all the other stuff on my bedside table, there's a notepad and biro. I start to make notes. I don't want to; I want to keep the whole experience as it is now, beyond words, a visceral part of me. But I feel compelled to get it down on paper. As I start putting it into words I can feel my recollection of the physical sensations dissolving. Words mark a divide between who I was there and who I am now. But my intellect needs to understand, it wants to make sense of things, describe it to itself, piece by piece, in words and concepts, slowly breaking down the whole into paragraphs and chapters. If I don't let my intellect analyse it, I will go crazy.

*

My parents arrive late in the afternoon of the same day and, after asking if I'm feeling better, start to tell me what happened from their perspective. How my father came to be sitting at my bedside when I came round.

Dad explains, "They called your mother when you vomited blood and she called me. I was closer, in Kew, so I got here first." He pauses, "Well, by the time I got here, with the traffic and all, you were already in Intensive Care."

I'm thinking it must have been over an hour between vomiting and coming round, drowning in my own blood. It must have taken ages for the hospital to track down my parents. Dad's still talking, "I couldn't come into the theatre but I could see you through the window. They'd given you blood but they'd put too much liquid in and it was coming out in your lungs."

"Yes I know."

"Do you remember?"

"Yes. It felt like I was drowning." Dad looks shocked, "We thought you were unconscious."

"No, I hit the panic button. That's what brought the nurses. And then my heart stopped."

My mother gives my father a look but I don't know what it means.

Dad says, "They were shocking you but your heart wouldn't start. You were white and I was sure you were dead."

"I was. I died."

They both look at each other again for a moment and ignore my remark. My mother, ever the practical nurse, explains, "They were giving you a diuretic, Forusemide, to clear the liquid in your lungs. Your father stood by helpless and watched as they shocked you and as your lungs cleared the shocks worked and your heart started beating again."

"How many times did they have to shock me?"

"I counted five times," says my father, "But I don't know, they'd already started when I got there."

My mother takes over their account, "When I arrived, your breathing was just picking up but you were a funny blue colour all over."

"So how long did they tell you my heart had stopped for?"

"The doctor said nine minutes from when they got you to the theatre."

"Yes, that's what he told me." It still sounds like an incredibly long time to be without oxygen.

When they've finished telling me their side of the story, neither of them asks me for mine. It's as if telling them I was conscious before the cardiac arrest was already more than they wanted to know. So I say nothing.

*

The next few days are spent in recovery. Before too long I'm back to normal. Doctors make tests, and I make pages of notes in my notepad. The urge to talk about what happened is overwhelming, but I remember the Light Beings' advice. Making notes is the next best thing. This way I'm only talking to myself.

The doctors give me a gastroscopy – a camera down my throat – and a barium swallow x-ray. They find lots of small ulcers in my stomach. As they're small, they think they have every chance of healing. But what caused the ulcers?

After the tests, mother arrives with a doctor in tow. He asks when I'd first noticed symptoms, anything like stomach pains, feeling tired, if I'd been ill or on medication. Before I can say a word mother speaks up for me, telling him I'd been off school a fortnight before with flu, drinking only lemon with honey and taking eight aspirins a day, the stated dose. Then she remembers our driving lesson a few days later when I'd felt faint and she'd had to take over and how I'd blacked out visiting my friends in traction after their bike accident.

For the doctor it all fits into place. He says he can't be a hundred per cent sure but it sounds like it was the aspirin.

"Aspirin?" Mother asks. "What's it got to do with aspirin?"

"Well aspirin has a history of causing stomach bleeding in certain cases, especially when taken on an empty stomach."

Mother begs to differ, "Well I've been in the nursing profession half my life and I've never heard of anything like that. I know aspirin can thin the blood, but cause stomach ulcers? I don't think so." She's being defensive, which for her, means going on the attack. I guess she feels responsible for my condition and there's something in that.

If she hadn't have been a nurse and hadn't thought she knew better, I would've got to hospital a lot sooner. But it's the aspirin that caused the ulcers that flooded my stomach with blood. And the nurses not monitoring my condition that inadvertently led to my heart stopping. Mother carries on as if I'm not there and now she's trying to put the blame on me, "He smokes and he drinks you know. Hasn't he told you? Couldn't it have something to do with that?"

"Well there's no evidence for that, that I know of," the doctor replies, trying to defend his diagnosis and play the diplomat at the same time.

He addresses me, "Do you smoke?"

I nod.

"And drink?"

"Yes, doctor."

He asks it as if it's something a doctor is supposed to ask. All doctors smoked and drank back then. Our family doctor chain-smokes in his surgery.

My doctor asks, "Are you going to stop smoking and drinking?" His head turned away from mother, he gives me a knowing smile and winks, making sure my mother doesn't notice.

I nod again, "Yes, doctor."

"My advice is, in future, don't take aspirin."

"Don't worry, I won't," I agree.

He turns back to mother, "We're going to keep him in for a week, ten days, monitor the situation," and then to me, "And give you a chance to get your strength back."

"Thanks," I say and, not having said what I really meant to say, "Thank you for bringing me back."

"Well it wasn't me, I wasn't on the ward when it happened, but I'll pass it on."

*

One day my sister arrives. She'd left home a year ago to start medical school, though considering how little we had to do with each other before then, I'd hardly noticed she'd gone. But she's still my sister and since what I've been through changes everything, I think I should be able to confide in her.

She sits stiffly, straight-backed on the chair, dressed like a woman in her forties though she's only a year older than me. She asks how I feel, adopting the formal tone of a doctor on her rounds. I sense I am a guinea pig for her to practise on. She wants to make a diagnosis so I start at the beginning with my cardiac arrest, how I left my body and found myself suspended, watching the nurses and doctor.

"John." She stops me in my tracks, "You know that couldn't have happened. It's medically impossible."

"But it did happen, I know it sounds weird but that's what happened."

"Well, you were unconscious at the time, so how do you know?"

"I wasn't unconscious at the time. My heart stopped. My brain stopped. I was outside…"

"You were unconscious," she talks over me, "You were in Intensive Care."

"I wasn't in Intensive Care, I was here in this room…"

There's no point in pursuing this. As the Light Beings warned me, people like my sister have fixed ideas. She can only see as far as the medical teaching she's adopted to explain the world and everything has to fit into that way of thinking.

"So why bother asking me what happened when you know everything already?" I'm being sarcastic.

"You're upset. You're weak. Things like that can't happen. You must have imagined it."

I'm not upset and I'm no longer weak. It's just her way of belittling anything I might say. Implying she knows my mind better than I do. So I leave it. There's no point. She talks about her studies, diseases, hospital procedures, just what I don't want to hear about. It's like we are complete strangers and the formality she imposes is stifling.

The next evening a nurse pokes her head around the door to check I'm decent. She says, "Two of your friends have come to see you."

It's my best mate, Nick. Here's someone I can talk to freely. He's with Jenny. They're holding hands, grinning at each other and at me like I should notice something.

Fuck, I think. My heart sinks. Nick and Jenny are together. It must have happened that night at the Jolly Brewers.

Back in the Light, everything had been so clear. I was in love with Jenny and all I had to do was tell her how I felt for everything to fall into place. Back in this world, things aren't so easy. I'm not about to tell her how I feel now she's picked my best mate. And there it is. I've returned from the Light bursting with the things I've learnt – the most important of which is how to love unconditionally – and I've lost it. I'm jealous.

I tell Nick and Jenny the details, about collapsing in the street on my way back from school, the bus ride, the weekend spent waiting in bed when I should have been in hospital. I tell them everything including the cardiac arrest and my heart stopping for nine minutes. But I hold back telling them about my beyond-death experience. That's what I've started to call it – beyond death.

I'm waiting to see if they'll ask me what being dead felt like. But they don't. They're too wrapped up in each other and what it's like as a couple to be doing a good thing together. Visiting John in hospital pays out more for them than it does for me. I feel mean spirited.

*

Over the next few days other mates visit. They take me for spins round the garden in a wheelchair. We have a laugh and things are getting back to normal. More than anything I want to tell them what happened to me but I don't. I'm beginning to understand the Light Being's advice. I know my friends too well. They'll just send up anything I say.

Three weeks after being admitted, I'm let out of hospital. After writing pages of notes to get it down fresh, and against all the advice of the Light Beings, I'm desperate to tell someone. It changes everything I'd ever learnt, imagined or experienced. There's so much new information to get my head around. I feel I've been granted an immense privilege; to know how life ends.

Just to start: existence continues after death. We each have an independent etheric consciousness that's older than we can possibly imagine. This material world is only one of many other dimensions that somehow create our dimension, though I've no idea how. How this one and that one fit together. It's impossible to keep all this to myself. I'm bursting to tell someone even if I'm met with disbelief.

I knock on my father's study door and enter. His study is overflowing with his two interests: mycology and property. He divides his time between the institute where he works and the Victorian houses he lets to students. For the last year he's been living in his study in the evenings, writing a book on mycology.

Desktops, shelves and cupboards are stacked with scientific papers, bags of coins from emptied electricity meters, magazines, fungal specimen in petri dishes, bills and receipts in bull-clips, old microscopes and magnifying glasses, all in chaotic disarray. He sits at his leather-lined Georgian partner's desk, writing under an angle poised spotlight, a fat cigar stub smouldering in his left hand. He lights a cigar at lunch in the pub with his work colleagues, smokes it on and off all afternoon and brings the stub home. I wait while he finishes a sentence and adjusts his reading glasses. He looks up.

"Dad?"

"Yes son."

"I need to talk about something. It's about what happened in hospital."

"Have a seat," he offers, pointing to a chair piled high with files. I clear the files on to the floor and sit down.

"You know when I came round I was trying to tell you something."

"Yes," he sounds apprehensive.

"Well, I've got to talk to you about what happened. I wasn't unconscious, I didn't lose consciousness, I left my body and I was looking down on myself from the ceiling, watching the nurses trying to resuscitate me."

He raises his eyebrows, "What do you mean, son?"

"Well, just that. I died and I knew I was dead and I went somewhere and things happened. A tunnel, a light that was loving and wise, unbelievably wise and full of love and I met, I don't know, not people or anything, but I met other beings like myself, disembodied beings and it was wonderful and…"

I haven't thought this through, I don't know where to start and talking about it out loud makes it sound even more fantastical than it does in my notes, especially compared to how normal it seemed while it was happening. In that other world everything made perfect sense. Now, using words to describe it makes it sound incredible. Words only describe normal things; things we all share.

My father looks doubting but gives me a chance to explain, sitting back in his seat, puffing on his cigar, letting me know I have his full attention.

"So tell me what happened, one bit at a time."

So I tell him, in detail, for half an hour. When I get to the demonic humans, I leave that bit out. It's not something I'd want to know about if I were in his position. I don't want to scare him or be responsible for putting thoughts in his head he might later have to dwell on. At least that's what I tell myself and as far as it goes, it's true. But underlying these thoughts is another reason. A deep sense of shame to have found myself stripped of all defences in the grip of such malevolent beings. My psyche was exposed, naked, and I don't want to admit to that. I'm like a boy who gets beaten up but doesn't want to tell anyone he lost a fight. In that world, it had felt ten times worse than that.

Through it all, my father nods and prompts but otherwise doesn't say a thing. When I've finished he coughs, relights his cigar stub, puffs on it for a minute keeping me waiting with baited breath for his response. But he doesn't have anything to say. He's stumped for words.

"Well John, I don't know what to say. That's fascinating. You sound convinced that that's what happened to you. I mean there's no point asking me what happens when you die, I don't know what happens – no one does – I really can't say. I believe that something must have happened to you. You sound so convinced."

I'm encouraged. My Dad has an open mind and I wait to see what he'll say next.

"But where's your proof? Anything that can't be proved empirically by many observers repeating the same experiments and producing the same results simply isn't scientific. If you want people to take you seriously, you'll need evidence. And I haven't a clue how you'd go about getting it."

I haven't a clue either. I feel crushed by the weight of science.

*

The next day my mother stops me on the stairs, carrying folded sheets, the creases ironed in.

"Your father tells me you imagined something happened to you while you were unconscious." I can already hear the way this conversation is going. I try anyway.

"That's right. What did he tell you?"

"Well, he told me you thought you'd died and that you had a dream that you went somewhere. He said you imagined you were looking down on yourself from the ceiling and that everything went black after that."

"Yes, that's how it started, but I didn't dream it and I didn't imagine it. It happened."

She cuts me off, "Your father told me. You know John, it couldn't really have happened. You were in a coma. The doctors were trying to resuscitate you. I've been a nurse all my life. I've seen lots of people resuscitated and none of them remembered anything from when they were in a coma."

"But I wasn't in a coma. When you're in a coma your heart is still beating isn't it? My heart stopped. I was brain dead but I remember exactly what happened."

She grits her teeth, a vein pulses in her neck.

"You were asleep for at least an hour after they brought you back from the emergency room. You had a dream. You dreamt it. That's all. I don't want to hear any more about it."

Her position made clear, she hands me the crisp sheets with ironed creases. "Take these upstairs with you."

No matter that we don't get on, this is so much bigger than that. I want to explain how my experience was as different from a dream as a dream is from being awake. I want to tell her the amazing things I discovered, what's out there and how it's changed everything I could possibly imagine.

It can't have been a dream that happened after I was resuscitated. The sequence of events was chronological and instantaneous. I escaped my body the moment I had the cardiac arrest and from that point on, one episode followed another sequentially. Dreams are muddled and vague, they jump from one scene to another. You can't connect them together afterwards. And the periphery of your vision is blurred while I could see so much clearer than when awake. In my beyond-death experience, the locations and atmosphere were constant in each dimension, and I'd never experienced such clarity, not only of vision but of thought as well, either awake or asleep. Then there was the certainty of knowledge and the hyper-reality. The wisdom, the love. Those new concepts couldn't possibly have come from out of my teenage subconscious.

More than anything, the litmus test of proof is this: however real a dream seems, as soon as we wake up, the first thing we realise is that we have been dreaming. When I woke up, the first thing I knew for sure was that this was no dream.

But I can't reason with my mother. My father has warned me about this. "Don't pick an argument with your mother. You'll never win." Overnight, she's made up her mind and there's no changing her opinion.

My parents don't mention it again, which means they don't want me to talk about it either. They want me to knuckle down for A-levels and get good grades for university. I haven't a clue what I want to do.

While they downplay the whole thing, I'm desperate to talk to someone who knows something about where I've been, some expert in the metaphysical universe but I can't imagine who. Everything's changed. It's like being hit with a sledgehammer and pretending nothing's happened. I remember the Light Beings' advice again: don't try and tell other people about their world, people won't want to hear.

But I want to hear; it's on my mind all the time. I decide to write up my notes for myself, for no one else. I want to get it all down while it's still fresh. I guess I won't be able to describe what happened in all its glory and brilliance but I have to try. I feel cement-fisted looking for the right words. It was beyond words, especially the conversations with the Light Beings. How to write answers to everything there is to know? I can only paraphrase.

It takes several hours late into the night on an A4 pad. And as I write, the same thing happens that happened in the ward. Every sentence takes something away from the visceral sensations of the experience. Turning it into words is like freezing something fluid or embalming something living. But I carry on, the next night and the next. I don't edit. I add but I don't subtract. Another night and I've run out of things to say or better ways to say them. My account is finished.

I file it away so I can face my mountain of revision. I've lost a month's revision time already and I've got no time to waste. After that, I don't know anymore. I've got a feeling this experience is going to affect my future in ways I can't possibly imagine.

The physical sensations of how it felt to be in the Light, surfing on the currents of love, begin to fade. I search for things in this world that remind me of that other world, only pale reflections but points of contact nonetheless.

I walk through continents of flowers in Kew Gardens, spend ages crouched on the slimy tidal walls of the Thames watching water flow, and stare at any cumulus clouds that float by. They are the closest natural phenomena I can find to the other world and on some days they're everywhere. In the public swimming pool I jump in the deep end, sink to the bottom, let my lungs empty and feel just a little how I felt when I was weightless in the clouds.

A map

Back at school in revision classes I find myself doodling in my exercise books. A white rectangle in a sea of black biro, a cloud of eggs drawn like negative frogspawn, circles of lights highlighted against black. Could this be a way of making sense of things, an illustration, maybe a diagram of the different places I've been? I scribble in the black areas trying to make the white stand out. No matter how much I fill in, the white never shines the way I want it too. Page after page become covered with more and more complex doodles.

What I really want is a *Boy's Own Handbook of How Things Are Made* with cross-section illustrations like those ones that show the workings of steam engines and hydroelectric power stations. Except I need one that shows how my consciousness fits my body, how it parted company and where it went. A map of this world and the next to chart my journey so I can trace my finger on the arrows that say *You Are Here* and *You Were There*.

How to draw a map of a metaphysical place? My doodles don't look like a map. Proper maps have borders and contours while mine hasn't any hills or valleys to guide me, or any horizon to line up ahead. And if it did, how would I place the map in relation to where I started, in the hospital bed? If I can't locate the entrance, the rest has little point.

And that's just the space. Time brings with it a whole different problem. The clock stopped ticking in eternity. Sometimes my drawings look like a maze and sometimes like a layered cake. What's the scale? What's the key? If I had a compass its needle would spin and spin and never find north.

My doodles begin to look like the maps of mediaeval explorers marked with things like *Terra Incognita* and *Here be monsters, dragons, sciapods and monstrous races of men*.

Although I don't want to admit it, I'm driven by something other than curiosity. The monsters of mediaeval maps are nothing compared to the demonic humans I encountered in the Dark. I'm terrified that if I can't find out where I took a wrong turn last time, I might have to fight the demons all over again. I want my map to chart a route around the monsters next time, as the one thing I know for sure is there's definitely going to be a next time. And if I get lost again, I might not be rescued in time.

New perspectives

Leaving school to catch the bus, I find myself standing at the same spot where I collapsed. It feels like a lifetime ago. In the cracks between the paving stones the bugs are still crawling through a landscape of dirt in their own tiny universe. There's nothing to see here. I don't know why I've stopped.

Walking to the traffic lights I feel like I'm the only person on the planet who gets it. It's not an arrogant or superior feeling, just the opposite. If I'm the only one who remembers the metaphysical world, I'm as alone on the surface of this planet as I was when I was lost in the grey mist. It isolates me from everyone else.

But isn't the same thing true for all of us? Aren't we all locked inside our own bodies, rooted in our own capsules of space and time? We're all looking for something to insulate ourselves from the realities of life. Things like work, family, friends, wealth, possessions; more than anything else, purpose and meaning. In one way or another we are all searching for something we can call truth. Ideas that will one way or another protect us, not only from life but, ultimately, from the unknown: death.

Well, I've returned from death and I'm trying to get my head around my new existential perspective. Trying to make the metaphysical and physical mesh together and rediscover my place in this world. We don't all simply belong to the same species – that's just our biology. Something else links us together. We're all part of the same mass of energy. It's as if each of us is a resistor in a giant circuit board with electricity flowing between us. But if the current gets too charged, a magnetic repulsion pushes us apart. What is the force we all share? It's not physical. It's the physical world that separates us. It must be the force that remained when I left my body. That was consciousness.

In the metaphysical world only consciousness remained. Feelings were a crucial part of that consciousness, both in the Light and in the Dark. On my journey through the void, scenes from my life appeared on screens and the emotions that were attached to each scene were the most memorable part. And in my life review with the Light Beings, it was the way I'd made other people feel that they most wanted me to see.

But what does it all mean in this world? Am I supposed to try and love everybody no matter how they behave? After all, I'm not Jesus, and look what happened to him.

The sun comes out from behind a cloud and I stare at it for a few seconds before my eyes tear up and I'm forced to squint. Why is the light from the sun is so painful when the Light which was a thousand times stronger wasn't blinding at all?

*

The recession is biting hard but I've never seen the High Street so busy. Posters shout from shop windows, big red letters on white backgrounds: Closing Down, Half Price Sale, Final Offers, Everything Must Go. People fight over bargains pushing and shoving to get the cheapest fridge, washing machine, stereo, TV. I overhear snippets of conversation,

"Go on. Get it. Look, there's only three left!"

"I've always wanted one of those and we've never been able to afford it."

"Who would think it? A Hoover for that price!"

A gaggle of girls stops abruptly at a display of knockdown fashions, causing a logjam. "Look at the price of those jumpsuits. And the tube tops. That's so cheap!"

A family of five, all walking abreast, sweep me off the pavement. "Make way, make way," commands the head of the family.

A mother uses her pram as a battering ram spilling people left and right. The shoppers compete for their own tiny square of pavement. Shopping is all that matters to them. I'm just an obstacle in their way.

I don't belong here. I belong in the Light.

I sit on a bench in the churchyard and take a backseat to watch the shoppers charging past like migrating wildebeest. I try to visualise them as light globes of consciousness swept along in the current from the Source, but the idea's absurd, ludicrous. Do they even know they're alive?

The Light Beings showed me a waterfall of souls cascading back into this world. The souls were choosing to reincarnate but by the time they arrived they were as ignorant as an atom.

I imagine what the world would be like if we could all remember where we came from. Consumers wouldn't chase knockdown goods – shopping means nothing in the Light. Having more possessions than your neighbour wouldn't make you feel any better about yourself. People wouldn't build walls around themselves; they'd welcome others in.

Why do we forget? I rack my brains trying to remember why the Light Beings told me there were things I wouldn't be able to recall. It had something to do with free will but I haven't a clue what. It's like I've just stepped out of Charon's ferry after crossing the River of Forgetting. I've lost everything I learnt.

I imagine floating up to cloud level and looking down on myself, sitting on the bench. From this imagined perspective, the streets appear to be veins trafficking schoolboys in their blazers like red corpuscles. And that's how I feel, a red corpuscle in the arteries of suburbia. My new perspective isn't doing me much good. I've experienced what it feels like to be a glimmer of light in the middle of the whole of infinity in all its incomprehensible vastness. But back here on the high street I feel exposed.

A month ago, blinded by my teenage ego, I felt invincible and at the centre of my own universe. Now I know that I really *am* invincible, even beyond death, but I feel as fragile as a moth.

With all this to think about, I'm weighed down with the pointlessness of A-levels, now just a few weeks away. The geography I've learnt in the classroom can't map where I've been. The history lessons can't explain the way of the world. Nothing I've read in English can describe what I've seen. The world constructed by my teachers is made of Plasticine and Lego compared to the Light.

For years my parents have drilled it into me that I have to be 'better than the rest'. I'm from a common junior school and I've got to be better than the prep school boys from private schools if I want to get ahead. But I don't know what 'getting ahead' means anymore. I don't know if I want to spend my life competing anyway.

My priorities have changed. The business of Kingston Grammar School, beating my friends to the best place, careers to be won at someone else's expense, profit at someone else's loss, these things which never sat comfortably with me are now impossible to live with.

*

One evening sticks in my mind from when I was thirteen years old – an evening that determined the next few years of my schooling. My father is badgering me to choose my O-level subjects, "You've got to decide what you're going to do with your life or you'll just become another waster."

I don't want to become a waster but I don't want to decide right then and there what I'll be doing for the rest of my life. I'm too young. I reckon I've got the time to wait, but he thinks the time to choose is now.

"You've got to make something of yourself. You can't sit around waiting for someone else to call the shots." He's been drinking and he's intimidating in a strop. I don't feel like I've been sitting around doing nothing and I don't know anyone else who is calling the shots, except for him and my mother.

"But you know what I want to do… I want to be an artist."

My father throws a fit. "You can't go to Art College. I won't let you. Bunch of wasters. Art Colleges are full of homosexuals and lefties. What's art ever done for us?" I don't know what art has ever done for us, or what homosexuals or lefties have to do with it either. So, to placate him, I say I want to become a biologist, thinking he'll be pleased his son is following in his footsteps. It's not an idle whim. I've thought it through. Dad's taught me all the names of plants and trees in the garden, both common and Latin names, then all the names of woodland and heath and some of the fungi that grow in them. He picks fungi off trees on forays with amateur mycologists and gets me to drink the white liquid that oozes out of them, to prove they're not poisonous and to entertain the amateurs as I scrunch up my face in disgust.

We've talked before about me becoming a biologist but apparently he's forgotten.

"You can't do biology, John." Dad sighs, exasperated, "There's no future in it, I should know. Everything's been discovered. You can't make your name in that."

Ironically it's my love of biology, of Nature in all its creative abundance that saved me from the clutches of the demonic humans.

The two of us are talking in my bedroom. No one talks about themselves openly in our family. Conversations around the dinner table are about things on Radio 4, outside of our four walls: the collapsing government, rising petrol prices, power cuts and the three-day working week. Inside our four walls, talking about personal matters is a private thing. Either with my dad or with mother, never both together. Secret one-to-ones like this one in my bedroom, or in the car, or, my mother's favourite, in the bathroom while I clean my teeth, her chance to put bedtime thoughts in my head.

Dad has a point about biology. The world of cataloguing species and preserving dead specimens in formaldehyde is over. There's an emerging new biology, the study of animal behaviour in its natural environment, not dead in formaldehyde, but Dad can't see it. Neither can I yet; I'm thirteen. But the science of ecology is just around the corner. It's the science of the interconnectedness of all things, like I discovered in the Light, not the science of isolation that my father's generation studied.

"Have you thought about electronics?"

I haven't.

"Electronics are the new way forwards."

"What's electronics?" I ask, "Is it like wiring houses?" something I've helped him with evening and weekend on his bed-sits.

"No John. That's electrics." He can't understand how his son can be so dim. "Electronics is going to take over the world." He knows there are careers to be made, but he doesn't quite know how. The first electronic calculators are just appearing in the shops but the word 'computer' isn't in his vocabulary. I can't imagine anything further removed from my sense of being alive than pushing buttons on circuit boards. Just the thought of it is soul destroying.

We reach a compromise. I'm fascinated by archaeology. On holidays with my parents I cycle round the countryside by myself, searching out Neolithic stone circles, round barrows and long barrows on Ordnance Survey Maps. Leaving my bike in a bush, I climb up hills to photograph them on my Exakta 35mm camera. My favourite tombs are the ones you can crawl inside under giant slabs of granite balanced for thousands of years on the precarious points of standing stones. I lie on my back staring up at ceilings of rock.

It isn't so much the science of archaeology that interests me as what skeletons and grave goods might be interred inside the tombs. Who were these people? How did they think? The sun and moon worship at the equinoxes, the lunar cycles, the tribes and their rituals... my imagination bringing to life the people of the distant past.

It looks to me like prehistoric man had a much better handle on the metaphysical universe than we do now. Archaeologists studying the past and anthropologists studying present-day so-called 'primitive' cultures find that animism is the spiritual bedrock of ancient societies. Every life form, every glade and waterfall, every great tree or significant outcrop of rock has its own spirit. Man's very existence depends on maintaining and nurturing these spirits.

And here I am, back from the metaphysical world with first hand knowledge and I too am an animist; everything in nature really does have its own spirit. Maybe that's our job in this world, to nurture and to balance the creative manifestations of Nature, the same thing our ancestors did for tens of thousands of years, instead of reaping the natural world for profit.

But I'm not thinking like this, aged thirteen. I reckon I'm not thinking very much at all, seeing as my parents and teachers get to make all my decisions for me. When I bring up my interest in archaeology with my father that night in my bedroom, without a thought he says, "Alright then, archaeology it is." He's lost patience with his son. I won't do what he wants and become something in electronics. But I don't know if I want to spend my life digging up the past either – I hang my head and say nothing.

Later that same night, brushing my teeth in the bathroom, mother comes in. "We've been discussing your future and we've decided if you want to study archaeology, then you'd better choose Latin and Ancient Greek. Your sister's doing sciences so you'll do classics."

But I like science and I haven't a clue what classics is. I spit toothpaste into the basin and ask "What about carbon 14 dating?"

I've seen the new dating techniques on TV. "Don't I need biology and chemistry to do archaeology?"

"Well you can't do both sciences and classics, your school curriculum doesn't allow it." And that's how I spend the next three years taking 11 O-levels: five more than I need and none of them in art, wondering how Ancient Greek is going to help me date prehistoric bones.

Now, after what I've been through, archaeology really does look like a dead end subject, but with university applications filed and conditional offers in place, my life's already been mapped out for me.

*

The crowds of shoppers are thinning as the high street closes for another day. I get up off my bench in the churchyard and walk to the bus stop. There's an unbridgeable chasm between where I've been and where I am. A yawning rift in reality and I'm not sure which side I belong on: neither, by the looks of it. I don't get the world anymore. When I stop to think about it, we're all locked in lifecycles that endlessly repeat and repeat. Our history master taught us that we learn about the past in order not to repeat the same mistakes in the future; I've always had an inkling that was rubbish, but now I know it for sure. The lesson of history is this: we repeat the same mistakes over and over again and the only mystery is why we never learn any better. From the ancient Egyptians, Assyrians and Babylonians, all the way through to the Romans and Anglo-Saxons, to the Victorians and the present day, mistake after mistake after mistake.

The only difference is that now there are more of us. We are getting bigger and living longer. We're finding things out faster and faster but apparently learning less and less. Our ability to do good is matched by an equal and opposite drive to do bad. And we're getting more efficient at doing both. These days, the material world is all that seems to matter. I remember a teacher in General Studies quoting from an article written by a retail analyst in praise of consumerism: "Our enormously productive economy demands that we make consumption our way of life, that we convert the buying and use of goods into rituals, that we seek our spiritual satisfaction and our ego satisfaction in consumption. We need things to be consumed, burned up, worn out, replaced and discarded at an ever-increasing rate."

It rings true. The way they see it is that the whole of Nature is just another commodity to be exploited. Satisfying the ego has replaced any sense of spirituality. People worship possessions and define themselves by their buying power. Social status depends on it. We're supposed to be the most advanced society in human history, but looking down from my displaced perspective, we look more like termites ravaging the face of the planet. So much for the march of progress.

Greed and selfishness, money grabbing, cheating, climbing over one another in a race to the top, manipulating others for personal gain, exploiting those less savvy than themselves. These negative human traits are the exact opposite of what was important in the Light. Victories over others counted for nothing. The only things that mattered were wisdom and love. Both of which I've recently gained and from the looks of it, just as quickly lost.

And the patterns I'm seeing aren't only in the rise and fall of civilisations. They're small scale as well as large: inside families, generation after generation; inside ourselves, year after year. I know they're there but I can't see them clearly. Why are we born to repeat the same patterns over and over? That wasn't explained in the Light. Or was it, and I've forgotten one of the most important lessons?

Life's out there waiting to happen but I don't know how to live with my experience. There are far more important things to be doing than beating my friends at exams but I can't see what they are. I've been given a unique opportunity but don't know what to do with it.

The bus grinds down Richmond Road and my new perspective intrudes further on my thoughts. We pass the Hawker Siddeley aircraft factory but the jets parked outside no longer look sleek and sexy. The Harrier Jump Jet is only a bringer of death to the enemies of suburbia.

We pass FW Payne, the Crematorium. I watch the smoking chimney, the dead people burning right here, just off the High Street, next to the post office, two doors down from the butchers. People's lives going up in smoke and no one stops to look. It's very strange.

I think of the Victorians who despite all their hypocrisies at least gave death a proper place in their society. They embraced death as avidly as we shun it today. The dying were surrounded by their families, who hung on their every breath as if their last words might reveal a climactic testimony to the meaning of life. Needless to say, they didn't.

Their relatives cut locks of hair as keepsakes. Photographs, death masks and portraits were taken for mementoes. On Sundays, people didn't flock to shopping malls but promenaded around cemeteries in their funeral best. Anyone could tell at a glance from the outfits not only who was bereaved but also how long they had been in mourning.

I reckon I'd like to be Himalayan and have the funeral ushers leave my body high up in the mountains for vultures to pick clean. Apparently that's uncivilised but at least death has a central place in their lives. In suburban England we don't like to look at our mortality. We take it away and hide it behind closed doors. Clean it up in the morgue, sanitise it in the crematorium until all that's left is a column of smoke wafting across the rooftops of semi-detached suburbia. I wonder if that's so civilised.

It isn't really the bodies going up in smoke that's bothering me – that's neither here nor there. What's really bugging me is the need to talk to someone about something no one else wants to think about. The biggest taboo for the Victorians was talking about sex. Now we can't stop talking about sex while our biggest taboo is talking about death. Something that's become the most important thing in my life.

Richmond Park drifts by. The thickets of trees and open prairies of long grasses are physically solid, as undeniably real as ever but I feel disconnected from it all. Teenagers like me are getting on and off the bus. They fill the back of the upper deck but we don't talk to each other. We come from different schools. Why does that make us any different? Right now it's making me uncomfortable. I want to say hello, get to know them. We're on the same bus. I didn't use to feel like this. I used to think it was only old biddies half way to the loony bin that talked to strangers on buses. Now I'm asking myself if everyone ignored everyone else, would we exist at all?

I get it. It's only me who feels like this. It's only my own existence that's in question and it's me who needs reassurance not them. Without some sort of contact I feel like I'm losing touch with the world, disappearing back into the grey mist.

A chill in my bones makes me shiver like from the damp of a slowly drifting fog. I've died. I've been to the other side and come back. I've been to the place the Greeks call Hades, the Christians, Heaven and the Buddhists, Nirvana, and it wasn't like any of their predictions.

I've shaken off this mortal coil, peeled away the layers of accumulated character and returned to an essence, an essential core. I've met with pure, unconditional love and wisdom beyond expression. Death has no mystery for me. I should be sitting on cloud nine. Everything should be fantastic, but it isn't.

I've experienced what's outside of this existence, the metaphysical world in all its out-of-this-world brilliance, and now I'm back here living inside some sort of illusion. My world has been blown apart. I was happier living in ignorance. It's not right. It's unfair. I reckon I should be brimming over with inner peace and have the answers to all the big questions, but I don't. I've got more questions than answers.

I can't even say death holds no fear for me, as the prospect of getting lost in the realm of the dark again is terrifying. When all I knew was the physical world I relied on science for answers. Now I need science to answer metaphysical questions, I don't know if it's up to it.

Where is the Light, where is the Dark? What's in-between? What are these places? How did I exist as a mind detached from its body? How did I take my thoughts and feelings with me? What happened to time? What happened to space? Where did all the stuff go? And most important of all, how do I avoid getting caught by the demons next time round? These questions are screaming at me from every direction. Finding answers is all that matters.

The biggest obstacle to my quest is it has absolutely nothing to do with what I'm supposed to be doing, preparing for university. And now, more than ever, my choice of studying archaeology, history and philosophy seems more pointless than when I was thirteen. School, bus, home and revision, I'm functioning on autopilot while my mind is somewhere else, in wonder from my close encounter, asking myself big questions I can't answer. I go through the motions of revising to please parents and teachers while all I really want to do is to find my way back. I've just turned eighteen. My life is in front of me. But I feel exhausted. I've returned from the most wonderful world imaginable and find myself back on the same bus as everyone else. It makes me mad.

Eventually A-levels are over. It's the last day of school term. I stand with my mates in the high-fenced quadrangle where we play football. We throw our school caps, ties, blazers, shoes, in the air. We stomp on them as they land in the sand. At last I'm going to have time to myself. I want to stop the bus and get off. Sit somewhere for weeks, maybe months, while I try to get my head around it all.

Escaping gravity

I spend the summer three stories up a rickety ladder painting the windows on my parents' Edwardian house in Kew. I'm outdoors in the sun and I have the space and time to think things over before university starts. In the afternoons when I've finished for the day, I walk in the botanical gardens, ending up in the hothouses, my favorite haunt. I slip over the roped off spiral staircase, over the No Entry sign, climb on to the upper walkway and hang out in the canopy of tropical palms, alone and undisturbed. The barrier between skin and air disappears in the humidity and I feel like I'm floating in a disembodied state.

I'm trying to recapture a taste of what my journey felt like, but this is nothing like the out of body experience in the hospital ward; nothing as weird and incontrovertible as looking down on my own corpse.

I lie on the walkway and doze in the tropical heat, thinking about my incredible voyage, turning it over and over in my head. I'm wondering how to find links, however nebulous, back to my beyond-death experience when one day an advert in the back of a music paper grabs my attention. It's for hang gliding lessons in the countryside just outside London. Four weekends of training and then a test and a license to fly. Hang gliders have just arrived from America; it's the new thrill-seeking sport. I'm not seeking thrills, not after what I've just been through, but since I found myself flying weightless in the metaphysical clouds, I've wanted to get that feeling back.

Hang gliding will be physical obviously, not metaphysical, and I won't be able to beat gravity, but even so it might be some sort of connection. I talk Nick into signing up with me. For the next six weekends we drive down in an old VW split windscreen camper I've bought with my savings; my first car.

On the drive down, I ask Nick how things are going with Jenny. He clams shut. Something's not working out but he won't open up. Clearly Nick's besotted with Jenny and I understand why. I am too.

The second weekend, we take off. My first flight only lasts twenty or thirty seconds but that's enough. I'm hooked. First I have to stand on top of the practice hill, lift the dead weight of the hang glider's wing on its delta frame, push out the wing at just the right angle, and charge down the hill at a suicidal speed. Suddenly the wing catches the wind and *wooooosh*, the hang glider's weight completely reverses and lifts off by itself with me attached.

I'm flying, an inane grin spread across my face. I'm surging with adrenaline, I don't have time to think but in those few seconds I feel connected to everything. The hang glider's wing, the air, the land rushing past underneath my feet. It's all part of me and I'm part of it. I push the delta frame away from my body to gain height, a voice is shouting in my ear, "Right, Right," but what does it mean? Am I supposed to swing right or push away to the right, I can't remember which. A patchwork eiderdown of fields looms ahead but I know it isn't soft like a blanket and it's approaching too fast. I'm veering into a hillside. In a reflex action I lie prone and the next second crash head first into a wet cowpat. It stinks.

I get up cursing, wiping the shit off my face. I have to get this landing thing sorted out and follow the commands the instructor is shouting through the headphones in my helmet. But first I have to gather my wing, shoulder it and climb the half a mile back up the hill. I stop half way up to watch Nick wobbling like a flightless bird thrown through the air, this way, that way, his legs kicking underneath him. All of us beginners are doing it. Lift off is such a shock that our legs keep going. The instructor observes dryly in the headphones, "Ok, you can stop running now."

The practice hill is a gentle slope on our side and a sharp escarpment on the other. We think it's unfair we have to run down the hill and carry the hang glider back up. On the escarpment, the qualified fliers simply stand on the edge, angle their wings into the updraft deflecting off the wall of the hillside and gently lift off, an image of pure grace. We're boobies by comparison.

The prevailing winds blow from the side, rather than straight at us, so if we don't sharpen the wing's angle to compensate we're turned back into the hillside. Crashing into cowpats is fairly painless. The delta frame has two big plastic training wheels attached so as long as I'm lying prone when I crash, the glider skims along the wet turf. A month of weekends and a theoretical exam later, Nick and I graduate to the escarpment.

*

Standing on the edge, it's a long way down. If I angle the hang glider's wing incorrectly against the uplift and don't control the fine balance of forces then I'll fall. Broken limbs are the least I can expect. The sun has warmed the hayfields in the valley below, crows are circling and thermals are rising. The thermals are like huge blisters of hot air bursting off the fields, unpredictable and potentially dangerous. You can be soaring one minute and diving the next.

Rows of little puffy cumulus clouds float above us, forming a grid that fans out from the horizon. For today at least, I've got back the sense of invincibility I'd lost since my beyond-death experience. My whole being is connected to this moment: sun, thermals, landscape and clouds. Everything feels right. I keep the delta frame down close to me, feel the wind buffeting over the top of the wing and with a surge of adrenaline, I push out. I'm away. I feel a gust from the left as I rise and adjust for it. The people on the ground become stick figures, the fields a patchwork as I head for the clouds. I'm at one with the air currents pulling me higher and higher. The instructor barks in my headphones "You're too high, come down a bit," but from where I've been, what's too high to me? Caught on a thermal the wings have a life of their own, up and up, almost level with the cloud base. "Get down here now. That's an order." I let go the delta frame with one hand and pull the jack out of the radio. The instructor's voice cuts out. That's better. I'm alone, in silence, listening to the rush of air, circling round and round in long arcs climbing higher on the thermals.

The elation is fantastic. Adrenaline accelerates my senses. I'm reminded how it felt to be drawn through the vast doorway towards the metaphysical clouds, surfing on the love of the Light. At that point in my journey I was the only sentient being in the cosmos and that's how it feels now.

I'm soaring as high as a kite. A thought crosses my mind and makes me laugh – I've not felt so alive since I was dead. The closer I get to the clouds, the less crisply defined their outlines. Flying into them I'm wrapped in a mist of water vapour. I'm not really here to make a comparison with the metaphysical clouds – that's not what I'm expecting. The link with my beyond-death experience is more personal. It's the isolation and the danger, the pressing need to conquer my fear or be conquered by it. These are the things that are the same. I might have started out dreaming about the physical exhilaration of free flight but what I find is more insightful.

As I manipulate the wing against the air currents I'm discovering what it's like to be totally responsible for my life; to balance on a knife-edge between life and death. To put myself in a life-threatening situation that is completely under my control. Unlike the last time. That was completely out of my control.

My desire to return to the Light is sometimes so strong it's a physical pull. They've been times in the last few months I've thought about suicide and how I'd go about it. But I've an intuitive feeling that suicide isn't an option. Whatever my potential, it has to be lived out for its natural length. It wasn't anything the Light Beings communicated to me directly, or if it was, it was one of those lessons they'd told me I wouldn't be able to remember. Maybe all that's left of that lesson is this intuitive feeling. A feeling I can ignore if I want.

Soaring in the sky, suicide is now a very real option. It'd be so easy to let go of the delta frame and plummet to earth. I'm free to decide, but to have that freedom of choice is what decides it. It's what stops me letting go. There's no choice at all.

Back in the Light the idea of why I wouldn't be able to remember crucial pieces of the Light Beings advice was somehow linked to free will. Now I have the free will, I decide to stay here. Whatever the consequences of my beyond-death experience are going to be, that is the life I will live.

I don't know how long I've been flying but I start to feel guilty about Nick waiting for his turn down below. I pull the bar in, angle the wings down and descend. I haven't thought about landing. Now I've decided to live I might crash and kill myself anyway but when the ground rushes up it's easy. I push out at the last second to brake and land on my feet.

The instructor runs over. He's furious. "Right. You're banned. Get the fuck off my hill. Now. Move it." I think of pretending the radio cut out by itself but he says, "I saw you, you pulled your radio cord. You dumb bastard," and marches off. It's what I expected but it was worth every second.

Nick is awestruck. "Fucking hell man, do you know how long you were up there?"

"Not a clue."

"Twenty minutes at least. You've fucked it up for me now. He won't let us fly again."

I go talk to the instructor, "It wasn't my mate's fault. I got carried away." But he won't budge.

"I've seen nutters like you two before. You long haired freaks. Get a chance and there's no stopping you till you do yourself in and I lose my licence."

He has a point; there was no stopping me.

As far as hang gliding goes, I can't see where else to take it. I fly a few more times in other clubs, improving as I practice but I never fly that high into clouds. Nothing compares with that first time.

After all, I didn't start out wanting to be a glider, I had a different agenda and I'd found what I was looking for. Not so much a physical link with my beyond-death experience, but a philosophical one. I realise hang gliding isn't going to help me any further in my search and I lose interest. I have to find other places to look.

Kew Gardens

The first weekend in August I'm still painting windows while Nick and my other friends have gone to a football match. I'm trying to finish the job for my Dad before we all go off to Windsor Free Festival, the highlight of the summer. Saturday morning the phone rings, it's Jenny.

"Hi."

"Hi."

"What're you doing?" she asks.

"Still painting windows."

"Can I come over?"

"Yeah. Sure. When?"

"I'm down the road. Ten minutes?"

I feel a rush of excitement but stay cool, "Yeah. Great. See you in ten minutes."

Jenny has come over before with Nick and other friends from the Brewers but never by herself and now she's just down the road. In my excitement I don't stop to wonder why, busy getting cleaned up and changed. The doorbell rings and I jump down the stairs. Jenny looks stunning in her spangled T-shirt and loons.

"Hi."

"Hi. You coming in?"

"You want to go for a walk in Kew Gardens?" she asks.

We walk and talk in the sun. We stop to smoke a joint in a bamboo jungle from China and get lost in a forest of rhododendrons from Nepal. We watch the giant golden carp swimming lazily under the water lilies in the hothouse ponds, feed the oriental ducks on the lake with sandwiches from the café and end up in a secluded field of wild flowers. Jenny flings herself down in the poppies and cornflowers, stretches her arms above her head and basks in the sun, eyes closed. I watch her beautiful face for her to give me a sign and ache with longing for her beautiful body.

"John," she whispers.

"Yes." I whisper back.

I know she wants me to kiss her, something I've wanted to do for months and what I knew, lost in the mist, was the most heartfelt, important thing I've ever wanted to do. Now it's here, it's our time.

"John," she says it again. My name is a whisper on her breath.

But she's my best mate's girlfriend. I curse myself. We've been best mates since we were six. Nick's in love with her. He's obsessed, he's jealous, sometimes he can talk about nothing else. It's not making him happy, he swings between anger and despair, calling her all sorts of stuff one minute and blaming himself the next. And if she's making him so unhappy I figure he should leave her and here's a way to force it but I'm frozen with indecision. I fight my conscience, a conscience I never had to acknowledge before seeing my life review and experiencing the effects of my actions on others. I can't betray him. My conscience wins. I tickle Jenny's nose with a shaft of grass and the spell is broken. She opens her eyes, gets up abruptly in a huff, shakes herself off and says, "So where are we going next?"

Windsor Festival

Late August on a hot summer's day in a field next to Windsor Castle, Nick, Jenny and a gang of us from the Jolly Brewers are overloaded with rucksacks and tents looking for a place to camp. It's uncomfortable being with Nick, knowing that neither Jenny nor me are going to tell him about our walk in Kew Gardens, even though nothing technically happened. Now I'm wishing I hadn't been so noble and I might be here with Jenny instead of Nick. I kick myself for having grown a conscience.

As we pass one of the stages we stop to listen to a vicar in his dog collar speaking over the PA. He looks out of place in the small crowd of freaks and hippies gathered to listen.

"As those of you know who were here last year, The Windsor Free Festival isn't so much a pop music festival but a gathering of thousands of people, young and old, to experience for nine days the creation of a tent city of people who long to return to the simpler life of tribal concepts. This is an experiment in a new society of love and mutual cooperation, which functions as a model world where all differences of creed, colour and politics are non-existent." He gets an encouraging cheer from the crowd lying on the grass.

For the last three years, the organisers have chosen this common land, the Queen's back garden, as a deliberate snub to the establishment. Promoters, ticket sellers, band managers and security guards are nowhere to be seen. They're not needed. The only advice for attending a free festival is this: bring what you expect to find. It's just a field in the countryside, wide and open, with woods up the back and a park road along one side. But it's been transformed into a miniature utopia by our presence.

Rock bands and folk bands play on the stages, hippies are handing out free LSD, jeans are flared, hair is long, dope smoke wafts in the air, suntanned girls dance semi-naked in the sun. But behind the party atmosphere and chaotic appearance, underneath the skin of the festival we've all got the same feeling that we're doing something revolutionary. It's ramshackle, disorganised, haphazard and unpredictable, it's not 1967, it's 1974 but this is our Summer of Love.

Later, I read something the local vicar wrote in the free press: "While the world outside looked in and saw nothing but the stages from which blared rock music, those who penetrated deeper became aware that by comparison to what was actually taking place, the music was incidental."

We don't know it but we're in the middle of what's going to be labelled the alternative society. It's that time in the seventies when genuine social change seems possible. It looks like capitalism has had its day; every week there are more power-cuts, more strikes, more dissatisfaction with the status quo. Fairer solutions are just over the horizon. We're in a field of like-minded people in the middle of an alternative way of life.

We pitch camp on a hillock in a wild wood and look down through the trees. The festival pans out below us in all directions, a city of tents, tepees, geodesic domes, polythene shelters, camper vans, trucks and old buses. Marquees and makeshift stages appear as if from nowhere. Some stages are built from scaffolding, others are simply a flat bed truck with a generator. Stallholders circle the site and line the main thoroughfares trading clothes, giving away free food, and campaigning for support. We're at the birth of new grass root movements like Greenpeace and Friends of the Earth. The environmentalists, ecologists, nuclear protestors, feminists, gay rights activists, Marxists and all the other grass roots movements are here. Everyone from the White Panthers to the Divine Light Mission, from liberals to anarchists all share one thing in common: a desire to create a different way of life. One that is fairer, with more honest values between people, less greed, less selfishness, more cooperation, more love. All these things seem possible and inevitable to us. Our vision of the future is simply a matter of common sense.

After my experience the growth of the alternative society offers a hope for a new beginning, one in sync with what I've learnt on the other side. I reckon we must be part of an unstoppable wave. Fifteen thousand people spontaneously coming together can't possibly be wrong. I don't know it but in only a few years our ideals will be completely ridiculed.

The first afternoon, we explore, stopping to watch a couple of rock bands along the way. We browse books of alternative literature on bookstalls, talk to agitprop campaigners, try on clothes at ramshackle stalls and share free food. We muck in and help dig latrines. We listen to romantic poets, religious prophets, folk guitarists and prophesising freaks. We eye up girls and bake in the sun.

That night, we drink and smoke and dance erratically in the woods, torches burning on bamboo poles and later, exhausted, sit around our campfire – tents pitched in a semi circle all facing the flames. We make tea in one tin saucepan, baked beans in another and hold bread up to the fire on sticks to make toast, all the while swapping jokes and talking about the day's adventures late into the night. It's the perfect time, under the stars, to tell my friends about my experience. Only I don't.

How to tell it? That's a mystery. Even if I got it as right in the telling as the way I've written it down, which I know I won't, I feel sure they'll send it up. So I don't try. I'm enjoying everything just the way it is and want nothing in this magical evening to change. It feels like the festival can go on and on and never stop. We'll never have to go back to the so-called 'real world' to face all the expectations parents and teachers have loaded on us. Everyone is getting on. Everyone is contributing one way or another. It's a far more attractive reality than the world outside the park gates.

*

But next morning screams wake us. A line of riot police advances across the festival site, smashing everything in its path. They charge the sleeping tent city, full of hate for everything we stand for.

People wake to truncheons flailing through the canvas of their tents. I hear one policeman shout, "You're the fucking scum of the earth," as he smashes the windscreen of a campervan. There are those, braver than us, who try to resist and fall under the truncheons. One guy has his legs and arms grabbed by four coppers. They ram his head into the side of a police van. Mothers with toddlers try to reason with them. A pregnant girl is kicked in the stomach. Later we hear she's lost her baby. The police take pleasure in their work. The opportunity for violence is the only thing on their minds.

We are lucky. Camped deep in the middle of the wooded hill we have just a few minutes to pack our tents and cooking gear and bundle out through the back of the wood. We circle round and get on the road to the train station before the police reach us. It's the third year of the Windsor Free Festival, our first and last. The Queen's goodwill has expired.

Standing in Windsor Train Station that afternoon we see hundreds of casualties limping down the platform, some in tatters on improvised crutches, some with bandaged heads, knocked out teeth and arms in slings. The local vicar gave his blessing to an experiment in a new society of love and mutual cooperation, where all differences were non-existent. But he couldn't keep the forces of hate from our little utopia.

The problems of cartography

I've filled two exercise books with doodles and scribbles, diagrams, measurements and annotations, trying to map my experience. It's become an obsession and I'm not surprised. I desperately need a sense of perspective, both for the map and for my search.

The problem is, all the maps I'm looking at have an aerial perspective; they look down on things from above. I have no idea how to find an aerial perspective for an experience that played out entirely in some sort of immersive aether. Aside from the world of the demons, that is – that was the only part that was grounded. I look at flight maps for pilots, shipping charts for sea captains, sectional maps for geologists, each has it own clue, but none a solution.

Nosing through the archives in the local museum, I come across a collection of seventeenth century maps of coach journeys. Straight lines mark the distances between towns where stagecoaches made stops. There's a tiny picture of each town along the way and drawings of the countryside the coach passes through.

I draw a linear map of my journey adding pictures along the way. Each stop is a different location. The first stop is floating above my body and entering the grey mist and I draw it as the shortest distance on my map. Although in truth, that was the most significant part of the journey, how I could leave my body and past through a veil of mists. On one side of the mist is this world, on the other side, that world.

Drawing each episode of my journey on to separate leaves of tracing paper and piling them on top of each other, I can see through each stage into the next. It reminds me of passing through screen after screen of my life on the way to the Light. Could my journey have something to do with my own layers of consciousness? Since watching my memories disappear in the movie screens of my life review, bad experiences from my childhood, buried many years ago, have returned to the forefront of my mind. Have these negative experiences got something to do with the realm of negative energy? Later that summer, I'm forced to revisit these places.

Strict and Particular

The last thing I'm looking for is a religious explanation. There are plenty of those and as far as I know, they all want to be the only one. From where I'm standing, the afterlife can't be exclusive. I was an atheist when I arrived in the grey mist, and when the guardian rescued me from the realm of demons, I was an atheist still. If entrance into the Light depended on membership of one church or another I would never have been allowed in. There has to be room to accommodate everyone within the same plan or the afterlife wouldn't be universal. And it was just that. My experience of it was the very definition of universal.

I've strayed into metaphysical dimensions that the old religions reckon belong to them alone so I guess, from their perspective, entering the Light has to be called a religious experience. The Light, the clouds and the Light Beings can all be fitted on the same map as a Christian Heaven. But Jesus and Peter, Pearly Gates and streets paved with gold were nowhere to be seen. And the same is true of the demonic humans in the dark. I can picture them as a version of a Christian Hell but again, not inhabited by any of the characters associated with a Christian Hell. There was no Satan, no red devil with pointy ears, goat's feet and tail, forked tridents or sinners burning in Hell's fires. I didn't arrive in either a Christian Heaven or a Christian Hell.

If an atheist is someone who doesn't believe in deities then I must still be an atheist. I don't believe in God, The Lord, Jehovah, or any number of other divine beings from any other religion. The closest I came in my travels to anything like a supreme being was the Source. But the Source wasn't a deity. It was the River of Life, the powerhouse that generated the universe, and as far as I could fathom, it was One, a singularity, whatever that means?

How can I join a religion with ready-made answers, administered by preachers who haven't been to the same places I've been? It would be the opposite of my quest. That's why I have no one to share this with. I'm in a research group of one. I need a rational, scientific explanation for what I encountered, not one based on faith. How to approach the subject empirically? Instruments haven't been invented to measure where I've been. Where's my evidence? Who are my peer reviewers? This is a personal search. I don't know any passengers I can invite along.

The other reasons I am avoiding religion resurface later that summer, when my grandmother passes away. Along with an answer to why my own mother refused to listen when I tried to tell her what happened to me. I discover she's petrified I could be telling the truth.

*

My father's parents died before I was born so my only grandparents are on my mother's side. They live on the other side of the Thames in North London. George, my grandfather, is the caretaker of an Old Aged Pilgrim's Home and my grandmother, Edna, keeps house.

Late that summer after the Windsor Festival, George phones with news that Edna has been admitted to hospital. She's been ill for a long time and now she is on her deathbed. On the drive north, my guts turn as I think of all the times we've spent at my grandparents. I've always dreaded visiting them and for good reason.

George and Edna started out in a miserable, rain swept village on the edge of the Yorkshire moors. They were born into a non-conformist sect of Christianity, Strict and Particular Baptism, a religion as bleak and joyless as their environment. It suited the dreary high moors where it took root sometime in the seventeenth century. A Calvinist faith of abstinence of the flesh and slim sustenance for the spirit. Daily worship took place in cold granite chapels stripped bare of any colour, adornment or heating. When the Church offered George the caretaking job in the Old Aged Pilgrim's Home in London, they upped sticks and moved south leaving nothing of their rigid lives behind, especially not their religion.

The meanings of 'Strict' and 'Particular' were complicated. Strict because only they and their offspring were allowed into their church; Particular because no one but the Particular Baptists were going to be allowed into Heaven. As a kid I used to think that heaven would be a very empty place.

My grandparents brought their strict and particular ways into other parts of their lives too. Television was the work of the devil. They never went to the movies and alcohol never passed their lips. Hymns were the only music allowed, and the only news of the world outside of their chapel came from Radio 4.

Every day Edna and George tuned in, listening for signs of the arrival of The Four Horses of the Apocalypse. They lived with the certainty that Armageddon was imminent. Heaven was going to be their exclusive reward for a lifetime of penitence. Only they would ascend. Everyone else, the Protestants, the Methodists, the Baptists who were neither Strict nor Particular, along with a world full of Muslims, Hindus, Buddhists and all the other nonbelievers – me and my father included – were going to burn in Hellfire along with the most damned of all, the Catholics.

Sometime in my childhood I asked my mother, "Why do they hate Catholics so much?"

"Because they worship the Virgin Mary."

"But she's a saint isn't she?"

"A saint, yes, but the Catholics turned her into an idol and idolatry is the same as worshipping graven images."

"What's a graven image?"

"It's a statue of a god."

"What, like a crucifix?"

I didn't get it. But if their heaven was anything like them, they could count me out.

*

Edna wasn't the sort of grandmother any boy would wish for. Right from the start, as early as I can remember, she pretended I didn't exist. Aged two or three, my sister and I were left at our grandparent's flat in the Old Aged Pilgrim's Home. As soon as our parents had left I was totally ignored. While George was out at work, Edna lavished her attention on my sister and left me to my own devices. I remember being thirsty and asking for a drink the only way I knew how, "Water." No response. Maybe my grandmother couldn't hear me so I'd better shout. "Water!" Nothing. I stomped my feet and shouted louder. Edna grabbed me, walked me into the corridor and opened the coal cellar under the stairs. She pushed me in and shut the door. I started to cry. When she opened it again, ages later, I remember my sister grinning as she peeked out from behind my grandmother's skirts.

That was my earliest memory long before I had the words to express a memory or tell my parents what had happened. It had always been there in the back of my mind, along with all the other childhood memories I'd prefer not to think about. Buried for all those years until it came rushing back as I crashed through the last screen on my way to the doorway of Light. And now it lay unearthed, there was more history waiting to be exposed.

While Edna pampered my sister in the house and George was out, doing his rounds, I was left alone to roam the grounds and gardens of the Old Aged Pilgrim's Home. I toddled through unknown landscapes of hanging willows and towering pampas grass. I climbed mountainous rock gardens and crossed prairies of lawn encountering strange, wizened old people along the way who would give me sweets. I was curious and everything was wonderful and new. It was a big adventure.

According to my Dad, the next time they wanted to leave us in my grandparent's care, I kicked up a fuss and my parents stopped leaving me there. My sister continued staying with them and they continued to spoil her rotten. But whenever we visited as a family my grandmother refused point blank to talk to me.

By the time I was maybe five I understood what was going on, but not why. At teatime, if the bread and butter were at Edna's end of the table, she'd refuse to pass it to me. I had to ask my mother who would ask her mother and she'd pass it to my mother who would pass it to me. Edna snapped at my grandfather whenever he dared pass the pickled beetroot or boiled eggs or answer one of my questions. Normally my questions would hang in thin air, ignored. Why did Edna hate me so much?

I grew up, I got used to it and when I was old enough, my father tried to explain. "Your grandmother hates all men and that means boys too. She can't stand any man she can't control and despises any man she can. Men are to be pushed down, women, lifted up."

"But why?" I asked. In his stoic northern way of looking at the world he replied, "It's just the way she is. That's all there is to it. Some people you simply can't change."

He had changed my mother, or so he thought. He called it deprogramming the brainwashing of the Strict and Particular Baptists. He employed liberal applications of biology and booze, things she took to with the same enthusiasm she'd once had for her religion. 'The Selfish Gene' became her new bible and alcohol, her sacrament. Beer, wine, gin, she drank at any time of day.

She never let us forget where she came from and told and retold the stories of her unhappy childhood like religious parables; sitting through services in a freezing chapel every weekday, twice on Saturdays and three times on Sundays. How lucky we were she'd left her church behind.

From my own point of view however, I wasn't convinced my father's deprogramming had entirely worked. When we were alone and no one else was looking, my mother would kick off, sometimes violently, as if there were a few random circuits that hadn't been wiped clean. Just like her mother, the need to control men had never left her.

And here was the answer to why she refused to listen to my account of my beyond-death experience. Not only was it outside of her control, but it was also the last thing she wanted to have to think about. A life spent weaving her belief system into an evolutionary biologist's explanation of existence could unravel overnight. She'd be back in the church she'd worked so hard to leave. So I'm no longer surprised that the day after my father told her about my experience she'd spent the night pulling the threads apart and come to the only conclusion she could allow. It must have been a dream. That's all.

*

On depressing visits to the Old Aged Pilgrim's Home, Dad invented a game for him and me to annoy Edna. He took what small pleasure there was to be had in the humourless atmosphere of my grandparent's house by getting me to apply logical questions to the contradictions of their faith. He couldn't ask the questions himself –

Dad and Edna had long ago reached an uneasy truce not to talk to each other – but that rule didn't apply to me. So he set me up to ask the questions he was banned from asking.

According to the Strict and Particular Baptists, every word in the Bible was the Word of God and therefore indisputable, along with all the pronouncements of their ministers. One of their more bizarre beliefs concerned the age of the world. In the seventeenth century, Bishop Usher, an Irish Archbishop, counted back through the tribes of Israel in the Old Testament and arrived at the start date for Creation. God had created the world first thing on a Sunday morning, 23rd October 4004BC.

My father prompted me to ask – aged seven, playing with my plastic dinosaurs, "Granddad, if the world's only four thousand years old, when were the dinosaurs on earth?"

Aged eight, drawing in my colouring book, "Granddad, if the Bible is all God's work, how did he write it? With a pencil or a pen?"

Aged eleven, "Granddad, archaeologists have dated Stonehenge and it's 7,500 years old. Isn't that before the world was created?"

Aged thirteen, "Which Bible is the Word of God? Is it the English King James Bible of 1611 or the Latin Gutenberg Bible of 1455, or is it in the Dead Sea Scrolls? Aren't they all different?"

George fielded the questions as best he could, "Dinosaurs were placed there by the devil to deceive us."

"God's word is written in stone for Moses."

"Scientists are fallible. God is infallible."

"The word of Our Lord never changes, whoever translates it."

Having set me up in the first place, my father would step in and explain the flaws in the religious arguments, to me but really for their benefit, using scientific logic. Edna fumed in her armchair; her jaw clenched so tight I thought it would crack, veins standing out on her neck like taught ropes. She'd jump up and demand my mother follow her into the kitchen, slam the door and scream at her like a harpy. Bringing disbelievers into her house, raising children of the devil, that sort of thing.

I watched Edna with a child's logic. She spent so much time working on her own salvation I reckoned she should be the happiest person alive. But she wasn't at peace with herself. She gave the impression of being pious, devout and pure of soul while underneath was a mean and spiteful old crone, the exact opposite of who she pretended to be.

There was so much to understand about people. The things they did, the things they hid.

When they'd lived up on the Yorkshire moors Edna had spent her life damning her heathen neighbours, reserving particular venom for the pub. For generations in her family no one had touched a drop of alcohol. George had never been allowed into the pub, not even for a ginger beer. The villagers had turned their backs on them a long time ago.

Down in London, George only kept the faith for Edna's sake and, as I later discovered, found the love he was missing in the arms of a string of washerwomen who worked in the industrial-sized laundry of the Old Aged Pilgrim's Home.

*

For someone so committed to saving herself, so sure of her place in Heaven, Edna's death is a shocking business. By the time we arrive, she's been screaming hysterically for days. The hospital staff have given her a room to herself so other patients can have a bit of peace and quiet. She hasn't lost her marbles. She's completely compos mentis; lying in bed, clutching the sheets to her throat, white-knuckled, ranting and raving in terror. Every muscle of her face and neck is taught, rigid with fear. And the reason is she's convinced she's going to Hell. My mother tries to calm her, me standing behind my sister, my father waiting outside.

Suddenly it's obvious to me that this is one of the purposes of my experience. I'm compelled to try and help. No matter how mean and spiteful Edna's been to me, I need to tell her what I've learnt. How to let go. How to find the Light. And if it comes to the worst, and the dark forces she fears the most embrace her: how to ask for help.

The Dark isn't Hell as she sees it, but it's still there. There's no fire and brimstone, no carnival-red Satan. It's worse than that. Full of the vicious and spiteful demonic humans who have lost any chance of finding their way into the Light, who thrive on the dark as it feeds their hatred. I don't know how I found myself in that land but there's one thing I learnt and that is whatever hurt I suffered from Edna, I wouldn't wish that place on her or anyone else. If there's a use for my experience then this is it. To try and help someone find their own way into the Light.

I step up to the bed. For the first time since we've arrived, Edna realises I'm here. Her face contorts into a snarl. She screams at my mother, "Get him out! Get him out of here!"

My mother and sister physically push me out of the room and slam the door. It's the last time I see Edna alive. She dies the next day. I hope at peace, though I doubt it.

I'm overwhelmed because I wasn't able to help her. I feel like I've failed to exercise a responsibility that I've learnt from my own encounter with death.

Thinking everything over, I try and figure out what made Edna so hateful. She wasn't stupid and could have easily seen the flaws in her religion if only she'd chosen to look. But she chose not to. Her religion gave her the ammunition she wanted to control the people in her life. Not just the men – her husband, my father and me – but my mother too. She put the fear of God into her. And at the last hurdle her faith let her down. In the end she was possessed by the same fear of Hellfire that she had spent her life trying to implant in others.

The way I see it, Edna had pretended to be holier than thou, a loyal servant of her God, Jehovah, but underneath her mask she'd made the devil her ally. She invoked Satan to control everyone around her and deep inside her, in a place she would never look until it was too late, she knew it too.

So no church for me. I had enough of that hypocrisy as a kid. And now I've seen the other side, I don't need a religion to tell me what's waiting there. I want an explanation of my beyond-death experience based on fact, not faith. It's my rational side that's seeking answers. The mechanics, the engineering, the nuts and bolts, that's what occupies me.

The Natural Philosophers

Time refuses to stand still and before I know it I've left home and started University studying Archaeology, History and Philosophy. I can't see the point, but Art College is out of my reach and I haven't a clue what else to do.

So I sit in lectures taking down other people's opinions, not being asked about my own; it's just like school. And while I go through the motions, making notes, writing essays, my mind is somewhere else. Trying to trace a route between this world and the Light. Where's the line between the two? Is death the only border or are there other borders aside from death? I don't care that the Light Beings told me I couldn't return to their world until my time had come. I want my time *now*. But I don't want to have to die all over again to get there. My longing to return to the world of universal love and knowledge is an emptiness that nothing in this world can fill.

In the lecture theatre I sit as far back and as high up in the tiered seating as I can. It's the only place I feel comfortable. I don't know why – it's a gut feeling. One day I'm there in the back row steeling myself for another boring two hours of Philosophy. I'm thinking there's nothing here of any interest for me. I'm wrong.

The professor starts the day by reminding us of our assignments and then launches into his analysis of the first philosophers. He's a lot younger than I imagine a professor would be, especially one in philosophy and he's wearing a black polo neck, black jeans and loafers and not a tweed jacket with patched elbows as I expected. So much for my own projections. His mop of curly hair and big tortoiseshell glasses make him look like a cartoon character. I think he's new at this as he appears nervous but he's got a slight stutter and maybe it's just the stutter that's tripping him up.

"We tend to regard the philosophers of Ancient Greece as the founders of philosophy and that's where we'll start, though it's worth remembering that many of the concepts we're going to study had their precursors in older civilisations.

"To take just one example, the evidence suggests that Pythagoras, the father of mathematics, studied geometry in Babylon where he learnt the equation for the square of the hypotenuse in a right-angled triangle. We give Pythagoras the credit for this discovery but it was the Babylonians who discovered it first. Nowadays, we take the Greeks as our starting point and tend to disregard their forbears. Whether that's because earlier civilisations made no clear distinction between their philosophies and their mythologies or whether it's a result of our western centric viewpoint are issues I don't intend to address here.

"The early philosophers were obsessed with two fundamental questions: who are we, and where do we come from? We're going to start by addressing their search for rational answers to the mysteries of existence."

My ears prick up. Maybe this isn't going to be another dry lecture. I'm asking the same questions. I existed as a mind independent of my brain, so who am I? And I transcended the limitations of the physical world into another dimension outside of the world of matter, so where is it? What would the philosophers make of these questions? I listen more intently.

The professor continues, "The pre-Socratic philosophers were united by one common enquiry – the attempt to find universal principles that would explain life and the universe. Hence we know them as the Natural Philosophers. Before this time, the Ancient Greeks believed that Olympus was in the skies – the exclusive residence of the Pantheon of Gods – while humans, when they died, descended into the underworld, Hades.

"Around the 5th century BC, the Natural Philosophers set about tearing down Olympus, evicting Zeus and his family of gods and rebuilding a cosmos laid on rational foundations.

"It was a radical departure from thousands of years of mythology, but for a seafaring nation who traded with the many different civilisations of the Mediterranean, it was a logical one. The gods had lost their credibility. Xenophanes, from the Ionian Sea, near Samos, expressed this most succinctly. He noted that the gods of Greek mythology behaved in selfish, malicious and egotistical ways, in fact, much like humans. He pointed out that the gods were born and died, just like humans. They looked like humans and dressed the same too.

He dared to state the obvious – a blasphemy in its time – that humans had actually created the gods and made them in their own image. As a counterpoint, he compared the Greek gods with the gods of their trading partners."

The professor fumbles with his notes, looking for a quote, and reads it in an elevated voice,

"'Ethiopians say that their gods are flat-nosed and black, like the Ethiopians, while the Thracians say that theirs have blue eyes and red hair, like themselves. If cattle or horses had hands and could draw, they'd draw their gods like cattle and horses.'"

He clears his throat and continues,

"Xenophanes reasoned that there *had* to be supernatural forces guiding the universe, but that they weren't in Olympus. He proposed there was only one force, the World, a singularity embracing all things, a universal force of everything; matter and energy. It was spherical in form, like the universe, and had no resemblance to humans in its thoughts or actions. It didn't mimic human behaviour like the gods in Olympus had before. In fact 'It' didn't really care. The affairs of mankind were too trivial."

He adopts the stance of a Greek philosopher again and reads, "'It is all eyes and all ears, but does not breathe; it is the totality of mind and thought and is eternal.'"

I'm riveted. This is something I can relate to. Xenophanes was describing things I'd experienced first hand. The spherical, universal force of everything sounded like the Source of the River of Life which flowed out of the volcano of golden light. I'd felt its nature, its utter disinterest – neither benevolent nor malicious and so awesomely powerful that if the Light Beings hadn't been there, it would probably have annihilated me without even noticing. It was like Xenophanes described: 'One'; a singularity, but what does that mean?

The professor carries on, "The new philosophers were free to question everything previously explained away by the myths of the Gods. Their challenge was to answer these big questions without resorting to those myths."

I'm on the same quest.

"Observations of the natural world would provide the skeleton of facts for this new understanding and theories deduced from these observations would cloak the skeleton with truth. This was the beginning of empiricism: the philosophical belief that all knowledge is derived from the experience of the senses."

It was my senses that had continued after death and my experience that informed my new knowledge. Here were the first rationalists asking the same questions and proposing the same empirical methods I had been using. In my case, I was out of my body in a different dimension when I collected my observations. Does this count? I can't see why not. I was still an empiricist.

*

After the lecture, because I don't feel comfortable asking questions in front of the whole theatre, I approach the professor and ask him if he can explain more about a singularity. What is it? How does it work? He looks perplexed, "I'm glad you left it till the end of the lecture to ask me as there isn't an easy answer. This is one of the most difficult questions in philosophy. The answer is both simple and complex. We could spend a whole term on the definition of a singularity and still not reach a satisfactory conclusion. Walk with me."

We walk down corridors and across quadrangles and down more corridors before reaching his office door and he still hasn't managed to explain. By definition it's a state, fact, quality or condition of being singular. In physics it's an infinite value, the place where there's a breakdown in the geometrical structure of space and time. For instance, the centre of a black hole is a gravitational singularity, as was the moment just before the Big Bang. The professor stops outside his office door and looks at me.

"The truth is, we live in a world of duality, opposites, one thing balancing another, and therefore a singularity is a concept that defies our understanding. All we can do is define the fact that there is a concept of a singularity simply in order to demonstrate our ignorance."

"What about Xenophanes' singularity?"

"He was talking about the universe as a whole."

I'm none the wiser. The Source was a singularity. The Light Beings imparted that information to me. And it was also beyond understanding. For sure.

The amateur philosophers

Later that week, I'm in my room in the student hostels with Mark and Paula – both on the same philosophy course as me – and Linda, a third year psychology student. I can't say that Linda is my girlfriend, not yet, things are too early for that, but we met over drinks during Freshers' Week and it looks like we're going out. The four of us are passing joints around the room, having a stoned conversation about the latest assignment: A J Ayers, The Meaning of Theism: Is it possible to define metaphysics?

I'm talking about his argument from that day's lecture; whether or not metaphysical experiences can even exist.

"Ayers says it's impossible to believe in religion, that is you can't be a theist, without using metaphysical terms like God, Heaven or Nirvana and metaphysical terms are meaningless because they're 'metaphysical'. So according to him anything you say about God is meaningless."

I've only just started when Mark, a politics student taking philosophy classes, interrupts. "That's what I think. The best thing the lecturer said today was, 'Defining metaphysics is like a blind man in a dark room trying to find a hat that isn't there.'"

"OK," I say. This is going to be an uphill struggle, "But the way I see it is, metaphysical terms aren't meaningless. They mean as much or as little as any physical terms – table, chair, sadness, happiness – all the words we use to describe things and feelings, they're all just symbols. They communicate things we experience. Like, we can't use any words at all before we've learnt them and learnt to put them together with each experience we have."

They look blankly at me.

"But that doesn't mean we aren't experiencing. Like 'table' goes with a table and 'happiness' goes with a feeling of happiness but we can never know for sure if my happiness is the same as your happiness or even if you see the table the same way I do. Your table might be coloured by your own idea of what a table should look like.

It might be a good, functional table or a poor imitation of a table and the same is true of happiness."

"You know what?" says Mark, "A table is a table."

"Well when you were a toddler in your highchair you didn't know that the thing you were sitting at was a table did you. You had to learn the word for it." The image of Mark sitting in his highchair makes the girls giggle.

"So? That's why we learn words," says Mark missing the point.

I take a deep breath, "But words are just substitutes for our perceptions. We can only use words to describe things we have all perceived. That's why it's so difficult to find the words for metaphysical experiences. We have to share the same experiences before we can agree on the symbols to represent them and that's where Ayers is wrong. It's not the metaphysical experiences that don't exist, it's the language to describe them that doesn't exist."

Mark is still hung up on a table. He says, "A table is a table, that's all I need to know. God is an idea invented by man."

I side-step the problems of theism and ask, "And a table isn't also an invention?"

"A table is a thing, God is an idea."

"OK, happiness then. How do we know this idea we call 'happiness' is the same for all of us?"

"We don't. Happiness is a feeling," says Mark and smiles smugly. I get the feeling he's not disagreeing with the argument, just with me, whatever I might say.

"OK, but whether a feeling or a thing, we all have to agree on the words we use to express the concepts and the same is true of metaphysics. What's so different about metaphysics that Ayers can separate it from everything else?"

"I don't know. Do you?" Mark is baiting me. I try again, not for Mark's benefit but for my own. I'm still trying to understand if language really is limited to experiences we all share in common. I want to get it straight in my own head whether it might ever be possible to describe the unknown to an unknowing world, or if it's always going to be a waste of time.

"Words are just symbols and if we don't understand the things the symbols represent then they're meaningless. Try asking a foreigner for directions when you don't speak his language, or ask an

Aborigine for a cup of coffee when you don't know his word for 'coffee' or maybe he's never tasted it?

"Or it's like that Magritte painting, you know, a picture of a pipe with 'This is not a pipe', written underneath it. It isn't a pipe because it's only a picture of a pipe but we all recognise the concept of a pipe so we all accept that's what it is. That thing about the line between experience and intellectual interpretation is what the painting's all about. If an alien from Venus turned up in this room, would he know it was a pipe until he smoked it?"

Linda and Paula laugh.

"Deep, man," says Mark, sarcastically, bogarting the joint, "What's with all the metaphysics anyway? What I got from that lecture was I'm a 'no meaning' atheist, right."

"What's that?" asks Linda, though I suspect she knows already.

Mark takes the hook, "Someone asks me, 'Does God exist?' I say 'I don't know what you're talking about'. God, the afterlife, metaphysics, it's all got no meaning right? It's all mumbo-jumbo. It's only philosophers who ask those questions."

"And some religions," says Linda, dryly, "So why are you doing Philosophy anyway?"

"Don't ask me, I needed a third subject for my degree -- Politics, Economics and Philosophy." Mark explains.

I'm caught in a dilemma of my own making. I'm uncomfortable talking about my experience. Something like that has a way of becoming a label. But at the same time I feel compelled to try.

I dive in, "Well what happens if you die and find yourself still there?"

Mark retorts, "That's just a philosophical question, because no one knows."

"Well I had a heart attack in hospital eight months ago and according to the doctors I was dead for nine minutes but I wasn't. I was still there. I left my body and watched the nurses trying to resuscitate me and then I entered a completely different world. That's an experience Ayers would say is meaningless simply because it was metaphysical."

That's as much as I want to say.

"Wow," say Linda and Paula.

Mark says, "Spooky man," and sings the theme tune to the Twilight Zone – "*duhdeduhduh duhdeduhduh…*"

"What happened?" asks Paula.

From the corner of the room I can feel Linda's eyes on me.

"Lots happened but I don't know how to talk about it. It's too far out there. Language is only any good for things we share in common. No one I've met shares the same experience. It's like talking Venusian. Anyway, people will believe what they want and I don't want to be labelled a nutter."

"What do you mean?" asks Linda.

"That all I'll be known for is this weird guy who thinks he's come back from the dead."

Mark guffaws, "You're a nutter."

"See what I mean?" I say.

Mark smirks, "Don't worry man, we won't tell anyone."

"Yes you will."

Mark, "Of course I will," and cackles to himself.

I give him a look. Linda says, "Well there are accounts of saints ascending to heaven and then coming back."

Mark objects, "Yeah but the stories of saints are religious myths and religion is the opium of the masses, right. It's all bollocks."

I can tell Linda's patience is wearing thin. She says, "Not according to Pythagoras or Plato, or let me see, who else, Plotinus. They weren't saints. They weren't religious. They were all philosophers with their own rational ideas about metaphysics. You're supposed to be a philosophy student aren't you? That means you're supposed to be rational, ask questions not just decide everything's bollocks because it's not politics."

"Politics is the business of life," says Mark, as if that's all that matters.

Paula's been sitting on the futon listening to all this and saying nothing. Now she chips in, "Politics is the acquisition and application of power. Power corrupts and absolute power corrupts absolutely." We all look at her in astonishment, "I read it," she explains sheepishly.

Linda adds, "Politics is the business of greed, how people manipulate their way to power over others under the cover of working for the common good," she's getting antsy.

Mark the politician argues, "Where would we be without politicians running things for us?"

"Free to make our own choices." Paula's answer hangs in the room. I break the silence.

I ask Linda, "So what do the philosophers say?"

Linda isn't going to be drawn, "Read it up, I've spent three years on this, I'm not playing teacher to you lot. You've only been at it for a couple of months and you think you know everything. Well, there's no shortcut and once you get into it you'll find you know even less than you did when you started."

Paula and I laugh at her Socratic joke and Paula recites the quote from Socrates, "'One thing only I know and that is, I know nothing.'"

"That's philosophy for you," says Linda.

*

After Mark and Paula have left, Linda and I are in bed together. I'm building one last joint when Linda asks me, "Why didn't you tell me before, your heart stopped and you went somewhere? Stories like that are not unheard of."

"'Stories.'" I repeat. "That's one reason anyway. When you say 'stories' it already makes it sound like ...well... like a story. Different to what it is for me – a shocking, genuine experience I can't explain. That's one reason. Another is you'd think I was a nutter, the weird guy, you know, I don't want that label thank you. Mark's already going to spread it around campus that I'm this weirdo who claims he's come back from the dead."

"There's always someone looking to make a joke at someone else's expense."

"Yeah, I know. Why is that?" I ask.

"He's trying to pull Paula."

"Yeah I clocked that."

"Trying to make himself look more intelligent by making you look stupid."

"Does that sort of thing work on girls?"

"Some, but not Paula. She thinks he's a prick."

I laugh. "Yeah that's for sure – 'Politics and Economics' – I can see him in five years time handing out leaflets for the Conservative Club. He only smokes because he wants us to think he's cool. He doesn't get what it's about."

Linda says, "Mark enjoys making other people feel small. It makes him feel big."

"But Mark's point-scoring is so meaningless. There's a whole world outside this campus that knows nothing of us and we know nothing of it. And he's locked into this one-upmanship game in a tiny room in a student hostel, as if that's the most important thing in existence."

Linda thinks about this before she replies, "Maybe for humans it is the most important thing that exists... status in the tribe... position in the peer group... fighting for superiority over others... I dislike it as much as you do but it's everywhere you look. We're ruled by primitive emotions and we don't seem to be able to evolve past them."

Linda's verdict is gloomy. I get the idea that she's already found out more about the way of the world than she wants to know. I wonder if that's what psychology teaches you or if it's her own life that's taught her.

She says, "People like Mark are always the most conservative. They don't want things to be questioned. Behind their façade, they're cowards. Well, maybe not cowards, maybe just afraid. They find whatever benefits them the most and believe in that. Closed minds, no room for change."

"Control freaks?" I'm thinking of my mother and sister.

"Not really, more like people who've learnt how to act only from self interest and don't want their behaviour to be challenged. People who like solid frameworks, rules and regulations, not change and evolution."

"Who don't like their boundaries to be stretched?"

Linda agrees, "I think they settle early in life on what works best for them and spend the rest of their lives trying to stop the cement from cracking."

"Like rearranging the deck-chairs on the Titanic."

Linda laughs, "Yes, like that." And is then more serious, "I learnt in psychology that dismissing ideas outside of the accepted norm is one of the ways people like Mark police the social group. That's why he was disparaging of your ideas."

"Pointless talking to him about metaphysics then."

"Too far out there for Mark."

There's a pause in our conversation while I place a roach in the joint and Linda stares through the window into the night sky.

"Are you going to answer my question then?" Linda asks.

"I did. That's why I didn't tell you about dying. I reckoned you'd think I was crazy and then... how would I have got you into bed?"

Linda acts as if she's angry.

"What makes you think it was you got me into bed?"

"Duh... we're in bed?"

"And you think you did that do you? Because I'm just a helpless little girl with jelly for brains, right?"

"Right. Pretty much," I joke. She thumps me playfully. I laugh and thump her back. The rolling tray gets knocked aside.

*

After sex, smoking the joint, Linda says, "So?"

"So what?" I reply. "So turn out the lights? So was it good for you?" I'm being flippant.

"Stop it," she laughs. "You know what I mean."

So, as best I can, I relate my whole account including, when I get to it, the demonic humans. At first we're under the duvet, late night noises from the student halls percolate through the building. Then we're sitting up smoking another Thai stick, curtains drawn and window open on clouds lit by the moon's unearthly silver light.

Throughout my account Linda prompts, "Go on..." "And then?" but makes no other comment. When I've finished she looks at me through a long silence. There's more meaning in her silence than any words. Then she gives me the longest kiss.

While we're wrapped up in each other, the emptiness I've been feeling for so long has disappeared. For the first time, I've shared the whole experience with someone else. Linda hasn't derided or ridiculed, mocked or sneered. She has accepted my account at face value. That night I sleep dreamlessly for the first time in ages.

The father of mathematics

In the library I read up on the first philosopher Linda mentioned. Pythagoras drew a map of the cosmos containing ten heavenly bodies. First there was the earth, then the sun, moon, and five visible planets. Each planet was supported on a crystal sphere: one sphere inside the next, a sort of celestial scaffolding. The ninth crystal sphere was the dark canopy of space and beyond that, a world of celestial fires.

The ceiling of stars, glinting in the night sky, were holes in the canopy of space through which the celestial fires were visible. Beyond the celestial fires was the tenth realm, 'a world of infinite space and infinite air from which and into which the cosmos breathes and through which and by which only it lives.'

According to Pythagoras's model, that's where I ended up, in infinite space and air, 'from which and into which the cosmos breathes'. The idea reminds me of the golden river pouring out from the Source. The breath Pythagoras described could be the same as the current of the River of Life I witnessed.

It works for me as an idea, but as a description of my journey it doesn't work at all. The geography is all wrong. I didn't travel out beyond the furthest reaches of the solar system to get to the Light. I traveled through the black void for what seemed like eons as the tiny pinprick of light got bigger and bigger and eventually became the size of a planet. But even if I'd been rushing towards the doorway at the speed of light, in the time I was dead I wouldn't even have reached Jupiter before the doctors had resuscitated me.

I'm being far too literal and so was Pythagoras. My guess is that he located the celestial fire outside of the known solar system in order to put it beyond any place the Ancient Greeks knew about. But we're not Ancient Greeks and there's no place to hide a metaphysical universe in the physical universe, or astronomers would've found it by now. However unlikely, I find that idea appealing. Imagine one day an astronomer turning his telescope to an unknown region of stars and suddenly seeing the door into the afterlife. But it isn't like that. Even though time didn't behave in the same way as it does here, I just know I hadn't traveled through the solar system. And logically, why should I need to? The journey I took through the void into the Light doesn't need to be located in a physical space. The physical and metaphysical are dimensions apart.

Reading on, I discover why Linda mentioned Pythagoras. Like everyone else in school, I was taught that Pythagoras was the father of mathematics. His big idea was that the world was built on numbers. Maths was the language of Nature. The changing seasons, the orbits of the planets, the cycles of life and death were all built on numerical relationships.

But as it turns out, early accounts of his life mention nothing of mathematics. In his own time he was famous for his theories on the transmigration of the soul. Pythagoras was convinced he'd been given the gift of remembering his past lives as he traveled from one to the next.

He recalled that in one of his lives he was Euphorbus, a hero at the siege of Troy who was slain by a Trojan, Menelaus. In his next life, Euphorbus became a philosopher, Hermotimus. One day on his travels, Hermotimus arrived at a temple in Asia Minor. He recognised a shield hanging on the wall: his own shield from his previous life. Although he had no way of knowing it, the temple priests confirmed that it was indeed Euphorbus's shield, left as an offering by his killer, Menelaus. After Hermotimus, Pythagoras claimed he became Pyrrhus, a fisherman of Delos, and then finally Pythagoras.

I remember the waterfall of light globes cascading back into the earth – and Pythagoras describes the same process of reincarnation, except instead of forgetting his past lives he could remember who he had been the time before, and the time before that. He also believed in something called 'metempsychosis', the ability to choose whether you want to return as a human or an animal. One account has him admonishing a man for beating his dog saying, "That dog used to be a friend of mine!"

Recognising a dog as a previous friend sounds a bit far-fetched, even for me, but who am I to argue with the father of mathematics? It seems churlish that people remember the maths and not the metaphysics. But I can see why. It's more useful. You can build things with maths, there's no room for skepticism. It will take a different science to prove Pythagoras could be reincarnated many times over. Hard evidence is less easy to come by. There's too much room for skepticism. This is the problem with my own metaphysical quest.

A walk in the woods

Next time Linda and I talk about the philosophers we are walking through woods surrounding the campus. It's autumn. Thin clouds hang like a veil across the sky. In my enthusiasm I've forgotten she already knows what I've read and she's patient while I retell it. When I finish Linda smiles.
"You've been reading then."
"Yeah. Sorry you probably know all that."
"Not all." We walk, while I wait for her to continue. "I was thinking about what you told me the other night about your beyond-death experience and I wanted to ask you what you do with that."
"What do you mean?"
"Well you're someone that's happened to, you've died and come back from the dead, you've seen what's out there. I was thinking if that happened to me, what would I do with that?"
"It's hard to know what to do with it. It's so far out there. It's impossible to prove and so easy to ridicule. That's why I keep it to myself. But keeping it to myself doesn't mean it goes away. It affects my life every day for better or worse. Mostly it makes me question my actions in ways I never would have thought before it happened. And it forces me to search for answers I don't know I'll ever find."
Linda doesn't say anything for a minute or two and we kick through fallen leaves before she replies, "You reminded me of something I knew when I was really little. Something I forgot but my mother told me later. She said, when I was four I asked her when we had first met and she started to tell me the story of my birth and I stopped her, saying 'No, not that. Before. When I picked you as my mummy.' According to her I remembered being somewhere else and choosing her. And I still remembered it, aged four."
I feel a lurch in my stomach, I don't reply. As the yards pace by I find myself fighting an impulse I don't understand.
"You alright?' says Linda, "Have I said something wrong."

It's an impulse not to open up, "No, not at all. That's fantastic. We choose and you could remember choosing at that age, so young and somehow so old already."

The impulse I'm fighting is shame, as if what had happened to me was my fault; that, and the fear of losing Linda if I open up too much.

"So what's wrong?"

I've trusted Linda enough to tell her about my beyond-death experience. We've already travelled too far together for me to stop now. I take a deep breath.

"It's just, you reminded me of something my mother said to me when I was around five. It was something she said after I started talking again."

Linda looks at me questioning. "When you started talking again?"

"Yeah. I stopped talking for two years. My mother said, 'Maybe you just chose the wrong family to belong to'."

"Shit. Why did she say that? And why did you stop talking?"

"When I was three she grabbed me by my shoulders and shook me until it felt like my brains were coming out. And she screamed and screamed and wouldn't stop for ages. And when she finished, I stopped talking. I imagine some of what she was shouting was 'Shut up! Shut up!' again and again, though I don't remember the words, just the sensations. So I guess I did what I was told and shut up."

"You're mother sounds like a monster."

"Yeah but what can I do? She's my mother."

"And she didn't tell your father what she'd done?"

"No. He was working abroad and my sister was at our grandparents'. By the time he came back I hadn't talked for weeks and anyway, when he talked to me, my mother was staring at me, like, daring me to say something. She didn't have anything to worry about. You don't have the words at that age to explain anything. You just have the feelings. When people were around she'd be as nice as pie but when no one was looking she'd come up with new ways to get at me. Ways to bend me to her will."

"Bullies only bully in secret. And only pick on one person at a time. No witnesses, you see."

"I've never thought of that. I've never thought of her as a bully but I guess that's what she is. I reckon it's hard for a bloke to admit to being bullied by a woman, even if I was only a toddler when it started. Anyway, by the time I was eight or nine I heard somewhere about split personalities and that's how I learnt to get on with her. I decided she had a split personality and, like you say, I was careful not to incite 'the monster'."

Linda looks at me sympathetically.

"And didn't your father suspect something was going on?"

"I don't think he looked. Too busy with his work."

"Didn't you tell him what was happening when you were old enough?"

"No, it was pointless. I couldn't say anything. All through my childhood when I tried talking to my Dad about the things she'd get up to – temper tantrums or spitefulness or blaming me for things I hadn't done behind my back and keeping me in the dark about what she'd said – he'd ask her what had happened and she'd say I was making it up. 'I don't know why John's making up stories against me.' That's the sort of thing she'd say. She always had my sister on her side. She spoilt her, gave her everything she asked for."

"Your mum got to play the victim," says Linda, "That's what bullies do. When they're found out, they play the victim."

I realise I'd never thought of that either. Anger wells up inside me. All those years of my mother changing like a chameleon from vindictive to innocent, from bully to victim by turn, and me, having to live with it but blind to what she was up to. It's the insight I've needed. I've been holding on to all this anger inside me for years and now it's come to the surface I can't find a release. I want to lash out and punch my mother to kingdom come and her mother too. But I can't. I've been taught to control my feelings. I don't hit people. I can break my fist against a tree trunk as if that will show how manly I am, but I don't do that either. I roll a cigarette, my hands shaking and inhale deeply.

The nicotine hit combines with the anger and makes me dizzy. I sit down on the trunk of a fallen oak, its roots reaching up like giant arms into the sky. Plates of fungi sprout from its sides. Linda joins me, rolls herself a cigarette and waits for me to get over myself. The thought crosses my mind she is practising at being a psychologist; that this will end up in her thesis, but I don't care. It feels good to get it off my chest.

"The biggest mystery for me is the satisfaction my mother gets from behaving like that; given all the choices that we all have in life, why would she choose to live that way?

"I think the way she behaves is part of a pattern that goes back to her own mother and for all I know, her mother's mother and her mother before that, who knows how long these patterns have lasted and for how long they'll be passed on, mother to daughter? Maybe it has something to do with her church."

"Her church?"

"Yes, they belonged to this weird sect called Strict and Particular Baptists."

"Strict and Particular Baptists? What on earth are they?"

So I explain their beliefs and practices and how they despise anyone not from their Church and damn them to eternal Hellfire.

"Wow, that's really fucked up," says Linda, "And your mother is still religious?"

"No. My dad helped her escape with science and booze. But her mother still had a hold on her as strong as her Church. The way mother and daughter behave; that pattern is ingrained and there's nothing my dad can do about it. She controls him as much as she tries to control me."

"And where was your father in all this, aside from working abroad?"

"My father?" I have to think about where he is, in his head, "My father's a proud Yorkshire man. He taught me that feelings don't matter. He says feelings aren't real; they don't exist, only things matter. Things you can touch, feelings you can't. And, in my beyond-death experience, I discovered the opposite is true. Somehow, feelings are the lifeblood of existence, in ways I don't understand. The emotional interplay between people is crucial. It's emotions that stick with us after death, not bank accounts and houses."

"And you can't talk to him?"

"No. He isn't that sort of dad. When I think about it I reckon there are more things I can't talk to him about than things I can. He'll talk about science for hours. Science doesn't have feelings. His way of thinking is that you can't let other people get to you if you want to be a man. And that's how I learnt to behave. He's wrong of course. No man is an island. But a proud Yorkshire man like him comes pretty close."

Linda looks at me quizzically, "No man is an island?"

I start to recite verbatim.

"'No man is an island, entire of itself, each is a piece of the continent. A part of the main... Each man's death diminishes me. For I am involved in mankind. Therefore, send not to know for whom the bell tolls. It tolls for thee.'"

"You're into poetry?" Linda was incredulous.

"English Lit. A level."

I ask myself why John Donne has stuck in my memory when I've already forgotten most of everything else. It's because it means a lot. The best description I've heard of how I understand the cosmos to be constructed: each of us, part of the main continent of life, all joined together in a metaphysical grid.

The first cold northerly winds whip orange leaves around our feet as autumn turns to winter. Linda huddles against me. The thin cloud ceiling is streaked from a pale yellow sun. We finish our rollups and carry on walking.

"When I stopped talking, I waited two years for my mother to say she was sorry or for someone to ask me why I'd stopped and no one did, so I decided to start talking again. It was out of defeat. I knew by then that my mother wasn't going to admit to what she'd done and while I was mute she had me where she wanted me. She'd made it a battle of wills between herself and her three-year-old son. And I guess she won. Incredible, when you stop to think about it. A woman in her thirties picking a fight with a three year old."

We fall silent as we pass another couple strolling in the woods. Once they've past Linda encourages me, "Go on."

"When I started talking again, around five years old, she asked me why I'd stopped, as if she didn't know. I mean, she knew but I guess she wanted to know if I remembered. And something, some impulse I didn't understand, stopped me from telling her. Was it because I was too young to have the words I needed? Was it fear of her? I don't know, but I couldn't confront her. I said nothing and it felt like something broke inside me. Something that was solid and good was fractured."

"What a bitch," Linda exclaims.

"She put such store in telling the truth, not telling lies. But I knew it was her who was lying by not telling anyone what she'd done."

"You're right. That's the way it works. Lies take many forms and the easiest is simply not to speak about something you know you should own up to."

"That was when she said I'd chosen the wrong family to belong to. I never thought much about it, just her being spiteful and enjoying it. Another bad feeling I didn't understand. That is until the memory of her screaming at me came back in my beyond-death experience, fleetingly, in a rush, as I crashed through the screens of my life on the way to the Light. Not the words. The five-year-old didn't have the words, just the memory of the event and the impact of the feelings."

"Locked away."

"Yes. Early conditioning, locked away. You know what the Jesuits say, 'Give us a child for the first seven years and we'll give you the man,' a Jesuit for life."

Linda whispers under her breath, "Same as the rest of the Catholics."

I'm surprised, "You. A Catholic?"

I can't see into her eyes but arm in arm I can feel her tense, "Convent. Lapsed. 'Give us your soul and love us forever or we'll burn you for eternity in the fiery pit of Hell.' Some choice, huh?" she says bitterly, "But you believe it when you're a kid and all the grown ups tell you it's true."

"Tell me about it," I say ironically.

As we walk, wrapped together, I feel Linda suppress a snuffle. I hug her closer.

"Hey, that's enough about my childhood." I say, "I'm alright now." But I'm not and she knows it, and I know she knows it. And she isn't crying just for me but for some dark corridor I've opened into her past. And we both know I'm pretending to be cool and manly about my childhood, while really, I'm wondering if that's how the spiteful demonic humans found me. By tapping into a place of dark energy where the memories of a spiteful mother and grandmother continued to live. Memories I'd locked tightly shut somewhere deep inside my subconscious, in a box labelled, 'Here Be Monsters'.

The story of Er

I follow Linda's leads and start on the next philosopher. Plato observed that our natures are fundamentally dualistic. We have a body that grows from youth to old age but we are able to survey the world with a consciousness that remains constant. According to Plato this was an immortal soul. He reasoned that along with everything else in Nature, our bodies rot and decay so we must be imperfect. But instead of rotting away, Nature continued. Why hadn't it decayed a long time ago?

There must be a perfect, permanent reality that renews Nature, or so he thought, so that everything can remain the same – unlike the impermanence he saw all around him. He called this reality, the Realm of Reason.

Plato came up with the idea that there were unchanging natural moulds or forms that everything grew to emulate. Behind each form was a blueprint he called an 'Idea'. His theory was that as soon as the soul, in the realm of Ideas, wakes up in a human body it forgets all it knows. The human sees a tree and a vague recollection stirs its soul: a forgotten memory of the perfect tree it knew in the world of Ideas. The soul yearns to return to its true realm. Plato called this yearning 'Eros', meaning love. He said the soul longs to fly home on the wings of love to the world of ideas.

I find it fascinating. Plato's Realm of Ideas is the world of the Light Beings, full of the potential of everything. And he described the same things I'm feeling. The longing to return to the Light, a world of ideas, a place full of love that I know in the core of my being is Home.

Plato came up with an allegory for his take on human existence and we call it The Myth of the Cave. Humans everywhere are prisoners tied up inside a dark cave, watching a blank wall. They can only look straight ahead. Behind them, a fire burns and a procession of cut-out shapes of animals, trees and plants passes by in front of it. These shapes cast shadows on to the blank wall. The prisoners watch the shadows playing on the wall and try to guess what they are. The ones who can guess the names of the most shadows are thought to be the cleverest. They're the ones the others listen to. The shadows are all they've ever seen and this is their reality.

When one of the prisoners escapes, he sees the long procession of cut-outs passing in front of the fire and doesn't understand. He's ignorant because for him the shadows on the wall are more real than the cut-outs. Not surprisingly, when he reaches the mouth of the cave and emerges into sunlight he doesn't recognise anything at all. He can't identify real animals, trees and plants, as they all look so extraordinary compared to the shadows of their cut-out shapes. After a while, he begins to take it all in. He acclimatises. He is euphoric, realising for the first time that these are the true forms of the shadows cast on the blank wall. He returns inside the cave and excitedly describes to the other prisoners what's outside. No one believes him. They think he's stupid as all they can see is what they already know, the world in front of their eyes.

The allegory makes a big impression. I get it. I left the cave and entered the Light. I visited the Realm of Reason and now I've returned, only one person believes me. Linda. The rest, of course, think I'm a nutter.

Next, I find what Linda was hinting at but wanted me to find for myself. A tingle of electricity buzzes up my spine.

Plato interviewed a soldier, Er, whose corpse had been left with hundreds of others on the battlefield for twelve days in the blazing sun. But Er's body didn't rot like the rest. Soldiers were sent to collect the corpses and build a funeral pyre. Just before they lit the pyre, Er revived. He told Plato where he'd been: a mysterious place with two openings into the earth and two into the sky, like cavemouths. Judges sat at the openings ordering the good, moral soldiers to follow the openings into the sky and the immoral, into the earth. Er was told to wait and watch what happened in order to report back to humankind.

Souls arrived from the sky and camped on a meadow with the dead soldiers from the battlefield. Er sensed they had traveled very far to arrive at this rendezvous. Those who knew each other embraced and talked about events on earth and the things in the sky.

While the souls floating down from the sky reported wondrous sights and inconceivable beauty, others, already long dead, were climbing out from the depths of the earth desperate and haggard and reporting terrible experiences. They were required to pay penalty for their wicked deeds, ten times over the cost of their deeds on earth. Er was given to understand that there were some in the depths, tyrants and mass murderers, who would never pay the debt for their actions. While he watched, a group of them climbed up to the mouths of the lower caverns, trying to escape. There was a giant roar and huge fiery sentries threw them back into the abyss.

Er travelled through the openings into the sky and reached a column of light that extended through the sky and the earth, the colour of a rainbow brighter and purer than any he'd ever seen. In the middle of the column were chains holding together the circles of the universe, like the girders of a trireme. These girders supported nine cosmological spheres on which the stars and planets revolved. The circles of the universe were like the wheels of a spindle, one inside the next.

Here Er encountered the 'Lady of Necessity' and her sirens, who turned the wheels of the 'Spindle of Necessity' that supported the nine planetary spheres. The Lady of Necessity cast lots to waiting souls, each lot offering a different life and many more lots than the number of those waiting. The souls were instructed to choose their lots, but the Lady cautioned the first against being too hasty and the last not to despair of running out of choices as the lots left over might turn out to be better than the first. Er was not asked to choose as he was there only as an observer. One of the sirens explained to Er how this was the most critical moment.

He was told to watch 'what the effect of beauty is when combined with poverty or wealth in a particular soul and what are the good and evil consequences of noble and humble birth, of private and public station, of strength and weakness, of cleverness and dullness, and the operation of them when conjoined.'

The waiting soul 'will then look at the nature of the lots and from the consideration of all these qualities he will be able to determine which is the better and which is the worse. And so he will choose, giving the name of evil to the life which will make his soul more unjust, and good to the life which will make his soul more just; all else he will disregard. For we have seen and know that this is the best choice both in life and after death.'

If the waiting souls chose a just life, goodness and happiness would follow, but these qualities weren't necessarily combined with the most appealing lives. All the enticing combinations of wealth, beauty, fame and power were on offer but these were often allied with their opposites – evilness, selfishness, greed and injustice. Some would become wealthy but their wealth would impoverish others. Some would seek power, thinking they wanted to help people, but find themselves doing irredeemable wrong to others.

The souls which came from out of the sky often chose badly. One chose to be a powerful dictator, but on inspection realised he was destined to devour his own children. Instead of taking responsibility for his choice he berated the Lady of Necessity and her sirens for tricking him. But he hadn't listened to their advice.

Souls who emerged through the mouth of the earth after suffering their punishment were more circumspect, and searching among the lots, often found a better life. Some chose to be animals, some animals chose to be human. Good and evil were represented in equal measure whether an animal or a human.

Eventually only one soul was left who hadn't chosen. Searching through the remaining lots, he despaired of finding what he was looking for. When he found it he was delighted – the life of a private man who has no cares.

Er followed the souls across a barren, scorching plain. Arriving at a river, all except Er quenched their thirst, not knowing this was Lethe, the River of Forgetting. The souls fell asleep. In the night there was an earthquake and Er watched the souls being driven upwards, like shooting stars, to the forms into which they would reincarnate, remembering nothing. Er woke up on the funeral pyre, remembering everything.

I read Plato's account, perhaps the first account of a beyond-death experience in western civilisation, over and over again. It was astonishing to find links with my own experience across two and a half thousand years. The geography was different and the similes were from their time: triremes, the Greek battleships with three tiers of oars; wheels of spindles for weaving wool. But the same things in my experience were there in Er's, like the openings into the underworld and into the Light. In Er's version they were like cave mouths; in my version, a dark malevolent mass and a doorway of light. The Lady of Necessity and her sirens were like the circle of Light Beings who surrounded me. The lottery of human lives that Er had seen was the same as the ripples of choice in the lake of human potential that I had been invited to measure for myself.

Er wasn't allowed to choose. Neither was I. We had made our choices already. Er was told his mission was to report back to the living what he had seen while I was warned against this, "If you try and tell people about this place they won't believe you." I wonder if the Light Beings have given up on us.

Choices

I'm faced with a dilemma. No matter how hard I try and stay focussed, my search keeps drifting off course. I'm getting sidetracked by my own life. I'm supposed to be on a quest to locate the geography, describe the metaphysics and find the links between that other world and this. But my own history keeps getting in the way.

Before all this happened I knew there were things in my childhood I wasn't confronting and I was happy to ignore them. I looked to the future, not wanting to look at the past and not seeing what it had to do with the present. But it's not working. My past won't go away.

It came flooding back as I soared towards the Light. You can't change your past even as you relive it. It's stuck like the grooves of a record or frames of a film passing in front of a projector light, thousands and thousands of moments frozen in time. However much I'd like to, I can't edit my soul.

Worse still, I find myself having to deal with all the emotions my past is bringing up. They keep intruding into my search and I don't know why. I think it's a waste of time. It's all fucked up. What have my earliest memories got to do with my search? My grandmother's hatred of men. My mother's spitefulness and temper tantrums. How are these part of my investigation?

This dilemma has sparked another question that's bugging me. It's also got nothing to do with my quest, but it won't go away. The question is about freedom of choice, like Er's description of lots being cast, my experience of the lake of human potential, and Linda's description of choosing her mother before she was born. If it's true that we choose from a lottery of life before life even begins – and the evidence is stacking up – then why did I choose this life? Did I make a good or a bad choice? I don't want to tell Linda these thoughts. She really will think I'm a weirdo. I'm beginning to think that myself.

*

The third philosopher Linda recommended was an Egyptian who came to Rome in the second century AD. Plotinus' metaphysical ideas influenced the early Christians, Islamists and Pagans, though he himself didn't follow any religion. Like Xenophanes, he thought there existed a transcendental being he called the One whose emanations created the universe of both matter and logos or ideas.

Humankind and the whole of the universe is the by-product of this One – nothing more than that. This was no creator god who thought or intended anything. The existence of the universe or any consequences arising from its existence, like us, for instance, was immaterial to the One; something of no consequence.

Plotinus found a metaphor for the One in the sun. The sun radiates light but it doesn't cost the sun anything if some of the light falls on earth. It doesn't diminish the sun's power and it wasn't the sun's intention to shine on the earth. The One couldn't care less, it didn't even think – to think implies a thinker and a thought, two things distinct from each other. The One was just not like that. It was indivisible.

I was back trying to understand the nature of a singularity, something I found impossible to get my head around.

Also according to Plotinus, matter – the stuff we're made of – was all a long way away from the light, in the dark recesses of the universe. However, a tiny reflection of the sun, the soul, burnt inside all living things. He compared the soul to the moon, as the moon reflected the light of the sun in the same way in which he thought each soul, trapped inside matter, reflected the light of the One.

He reasoned that each soul creates the world by stepping from the One into Time. Time was crucial to the equation. But he couldn't explain what Time was. Plotinus thought that on death, the flickering light of the soul left the body and returned to the flames of the One. Apart from those who were too far away to find their way back.

I wondered what happened to those left in the dark, trapped forever with no chance of return. I had met them and they were the purest evil. Was there no chance of escape, ever? No opportunity to change their ways? Or were they like the souls emerging from the deep caves inside the earth, in Er's account, ready to choose new lives. Rescued like I had been in the arms of the guardian.

I wondered why I had found myself in the dark in the first place, with nothing I could see to blemish my copybook. Was it my arrogance, believing myself invincible? Surely every teenager feels like that. Or was it something rooted more deeply in the dark soil of my subconscious?

When I was in the clutches of the demons, I'd had the intuitive idea that the whole experience was energetic; that the demonic world was the product of negative energy. Maybe it wasn't only bad things people did in life that had to be resolved in death, like the immoral humans Er saw descending into the earth.

Not for the first time, I begin to wonder if it works another way. That bad things done to people, maybe bad things they've locked away in their subconscious and haven't faced up to can have the same effect. Was a residue of negative energy lying dormant from my childhood, something toxic like a bomb waiting to go off? When I was in the mist, was it this toxic time bomb that had attracted the forces of evil, opened a crack into their world and let them in?

And what if, before I was born, when I was like one of the souls Er watched picking up the lottery cards of life, what if I'd been in too much of a rush, I'd chosen too quickly and not considered the consequences till too late? What if my mother had been right all along and I had, in fact, chosen the wrong family to be born into?

Potential

Sometime in the autumn term, things start going wrong. The quiet of the lecture theatre makes me edgy. There are so many people crushed into the same space. No one talks except the professor. We don't even say hello when we first sit down. It feels unnatural. I remember sitting on the bus home from school surrounded by teenagers my own age but not talking, just because we came from different schools. It's like that. Unnerving. I am hanging on to reality and feel at any moment I might evaporate and disappear into a mist.

I'm slipping my moorings, floating away on a current. I can't shake the sensation. It's physical. It's got something to do with my beyond-death experience but I don't know what. If I'm right and we're all linked together like a wiring diagram then I'm short-circuiting. Or if everyone is insulated inside their own little bubble, my bubble must have burst.

Why is this happening? My life review took me back to my childhood and threw it into focus. Is it something to do with that? I was disembodied, lost in the mist, didn't know which way to turn. Is that it? Or maybe the demonic humans wounded my psyche in ways that have yet to heal. These are dark thoughts from dark places.

But maybe my sense of panic comes from the opposite side of my journey – an after effect, a flashback of the Light. Seeing as I had to relinquish my identity in order to enter the Light, maybe the layers of ego that cloaked my skeleton haven't quite grown back. Or seeing myself as a tiny dot against the background of infinity has blown my mind. I don't know, but all these possibilities are connected in some way.

Trying to work it out only makes it worse. I feel trapped, claustrophobic; my hands turn clammy, I break into a cold sweat, there's a whistling sound in my ears like a bomb about to land as the lecturer's voice fades into the distance. It feels like I'm becoming disembodied all over again, and I have to focus really hard to pull myself back together. After the first term, the thought of three years of this is too much. I can't handle it so I drop out of university.

*

I don't tell my parents why I've left. They wouldn't understand. It's to do with the things they refuse to recognise and they just assume I've become a dropout. It's not even a year since they almost lost their son but my mother doesn't want me back home, arguing with my dad till he gives in. He needs someone to manage the tenants in Kingston and he offers me a bedsit in return for running the house for him.

The bedsit is damp and gloomy. I'm in the basement with only a slit of light coming through a window set back underneath a balcony above; one room with a corner kitchenette, sharing a toilet and bathroom with three other tenants. I reckon my father could've offered me a better room than this after all the work I've done for him. It feels like he's got it in for me like my mother, but it's probably her doing. I'll just have to get by.

But I'm not going to live in the dark. I collect electric lights and bags of fifty pence pieces to feed the electricity meter. Old lights from junk shops in need of rewiring – an angle-poise, a dentist's light, photography studio lights – and modern ones from department stores – lava lamps and a spray of fibre optics that reminds me of the doorway in the void. On a cloudy day the bedsit is brighter than outside.

I sign on the dole. The recession is getting worse and jobs are thin on the ground. After a few weeks I take a job washing cars to tide me over. The work is mindless but it's outdoors and that's where I feel most comfortable. With no distractions I've finally found the space I need to try and get my head around what happened. But at what cost? University, family, friends, girlfriend? I could cry at the loss but I steel myself instead. I don't have a choice in the matter. One potential future has closed and another potential has opened in its place. This is where I stand. By myself in a car park in the middle of winter with a bucket of water and sponge.

The biggest thing that bugs me is why I had to come back at all? Why couldn't I have stayed in the Light where I belonged? The reason is obvious: the doctors resuscitated me. But it throws up the question as to whether or not the Light Beings had any influence over the events that were happening in the hospital theatre. They told me it wasn't my time and I had to go back, but could they have let me stay if they'd wanted to?

Does the world of the Light govern the world of matter or is it the other way round? Are the two worlds connected or simply parallel? While I was in the metaphysical world, the knowledge that the Light was the creator of this physical world was more certain than anything. The Source was the River of Life. Light comes before matter. But how do the two realities link up? I need to know for my map to make any sense. Washing cars is sheer drudgery, and questions like these keep my thoughts alive.

Whenever I'm back in my bedsit I sketch different ways the two worlds might fit together. I screw up drawing after drawing and start again. I've been drawing the physical universe inside the metaphysical, matter as a by-product of light, but seeing as the Light Beings didn't stop the doctors resuscitating me when I wanted so badly to stay in their world, maybe it's the other way round.

*

Back at the carwash, filling another bucket of hot water, I squirt in shampoo and dunk my sponge into the bubbles to soap another pool car. I wash the cars for sales reps selling aluminium beer barrels to breweries up and down the country. They bring the cars back covered in motorway grime. And while I'm scrubbing away at the dirt I think about what the Light Beings taught me. Lessons about love and wisdom, potential and compassion.

Love was central to everything. It was a vast, tangible, physical force, a sensation of positivity that buzzed through me and inside me, lifting my spirits and my awareness beyond anything it is possible to experience on earth. I was invincible. Not in the way I'd imagined myself last year as a naïve seventeen-year-old, but truly invincible in a literal way: an indestructible way. And this certainty was accompanied by the deepest knowledge that this state of consciousness was an essence that had existed for a very long time. These thoughts make my life washing cars in a car pool all the more meaningless. However much I want to re-experience that state of being, it's gone. So what can I expect from love in this world?

I think about Jenny. When I was hanging in the grey mist the feeling of unrequited love overwhelmed all the other feelings of loss; of the world, of life itself. It was the loneliest I'd ever felt and in that moment my love for Jenny was the most important thing. And now she's with Nick? The fact that I'm jealous tells me this sort of love can't be the same as the love I felt in the Light. This is egotistical. I want her to be mine.

Love for Linda? We've split up. I'm not surprised. We're separated by geography. We're still friends: I catch trains to her campus that's no longer my campus; she visits me in my basement bedsit that's no longer a world that appeals to her. Aside from the physical distance, I reckon I opened up too much. I'm learning there's only so much honesty a romance needs and only so much it can take. But I miss her and it's not just about the physical stuff.

Surely love for a life partner, a soul mate, must be the strongest link in life? But when I find someone to love who loves me back, what then? Can it last? I look at my parents. I imagine they must have been in love once upon a time. So how have they ended up spending their lives at different ends of the house? My mother hiding her alcoholism and her need to control the world, my father ignoring both. Keeping up appearances for so long has finally worn them out. The years have weathered their marriage and neither can see the erosion.

Why don't they get divorced? They've talked about it enough times. Or does being stronger together end up making you weaker by yourself? If that's what I have to look forward to, is relying on someone else really such a good thing?

I think about my parents' love for me. It's supposed to be constant and unconditional but the ties that bind my parents' love are knotted with judgement and conditions. I can't say I love my mother, nor she me. I love my father and I guess he loves me too but it's hard to find proof inside our relationship when he can't talk about it. It's not manly. Perhaps it's there, it's just not tangible after all the years he's spent making conditions – 'ifs' and 'whens' and 'woulds' and 'shoulds' – and his disappointment that his son isn't more like him.

Human love is turning out to be far more complicated than the energetic love of the Light. So are there other sorts of love to be found in this life?

My love of the natural world and the wonders of the cosmos was the very thing that brought the guardian to my side. It's a feeling that comes out of nowhere, by chance, and disappears just as mysteriously. It's a sense of wonder that is as likely to arrive from seeing a dew-covered spider-web or a leaf spiralling in the wind as from the sight of a canopy of stars. It goes hand in hand with knowledge and understanding. The problem is, if I try and project myself into that state of mind, nothing happens. Wishful thinking doesn't work. The thought is a thin reflection of the real feeling.

In the Light, the search for knowledge and understanding was inextricably linked to love. They had an intimate connection, but I've forgotten what that is. All that's left is a message that the search for wisdom and love is our most important goal in life. My beyond-death experience gave me a glimpse of that possibility. Now it's vanished.

The love of the Light was incomparable. Compassionate, accepting, unconditional and non-judgemental. It generated positivity, contentment, a sense of belonging and understanding: a wonderful sensation, one I can never forget. But it was also unearthly, so I have little chance of finding it in this life.

That doesn't mean I'm going to stop looking however. It's just that I don't know where to look. In the love of my parents that's so conditional, in my love of nature that's so ephemeral, in the love of a girlfriend that so far is either short-lived or unavailable? In all these thoughts I forget to question my love for myself. Squeezing out sponges of freezing water to rinse shampoo off car bodies, that's the one thing I seem to be lacking.

*

Next there's the question of potential. The Light Beings told me I wouldn't be able to remember the ripples in the lake of potential or even the reasons why I can't remember. So what was the point of them telling me in the first place? I remember their warnings about the choices I might have made in the past or will make in an unknown future. I remember the importance of exercising free will but nothing about why free will is important. I guess if you know what you're supposed to be doing and where it will lead, it will change the way your life plays out. But how will I know I'm making the right choices if I can't remember the first thing about their advice?

Hosing off a Hillman Hunter, with eleven O-levels and three A-levels behind me, it's pretty obvious I'm making the wrong choices already. It wasn't like I was handed any great mission or anything, like Er, who was told to report what he saw back to mankind. I didn't return with any sense of responsibility or self-importance, in fact it was just the opposite. What sense of self-importance I used to have has been squashed under the weight of infinity.

I don't know what success means anymore. I know it's not material. However much I'd like a nice house and a dependable car, to judge my value on the piles of stuff I can accumulate is irrelevant. And success isn't about having power over others, something Edna craved, but didn't make her happy.

Potential and compassion were somehow linked. When the Light Beings screened my life they weren't there to enforce some sort of metaphysical morality. They didn't judge me. It was me who judged myself by experiencing the consequences of my actions on others. Plus, in the Light, the effects were magnified, both good and bad.

Next time round, any dishonesty, trickery, meanness or malice will come back on me tenfold. I have a new sense of responsibility for how I behave. I'm going to try my hardest to tread carefully: I don't want to live to regret my actions in eternity. So how can I serve myself and not hurt others at the same time? It seems impossible. We're all self-centred and no more so then when we're young. It's a survival instinct.

I think of Jenny in Kew Gardens and how I bottled my desire for her because she was going out with my best friend. And how he knows nothing about it. Well, that was a shitty thing for me to do, and for Jenny too if she wanted me more than Nick, and a shitty situation either way for Nick. It's all way too complicated for me to get my head around. I kick myself for not having followed my heart.

Is it possible to live a spotless life? I haven't a clue. I curse the Light Beings for my new perspective while I don't even know if it's mine or theirs. It feels like they've infiltrated my psyche. I'm not even sure if the purpose of my life review was for my education anyway. Perhaps it wasn't a lesson they were teaching me but a lesson they were learning. Collecting all the tiny details of insignificant lives like mine together in their library. If I could see the library, perhaps it would all make sense.

Filling another bucket of water I start on the Director's wife's Alpha Romeo. That's a perk of the Director's job. To have the help clean his wife's car. It sucks.

I want to believe that in the greater scheme of things nothing really matters. But I've seen the greater scheme of things and I know it does. Every damn little thing.

My thoughts stop abruptly as if they've run out of line and need reeling in. I've just remembered what the Light Beings showed me. The importance of compassion; how tiny acts of kindness I'd shown towards others had made them feel better. It might not be much, but to the Light Beings it was all-important. If success has something to do with having compassion for others then I'll try putting myself in other people's shoes and looking at things from the their point of view.

As I finish up by polishing the Finance Director's Vanden Plas Jag, I reflect that however vague my memories of the lake of potential might be, nothing means more to me than the experience of the Light. The love and wisdom, the indisputable knowledge that I had arrived Home. I want to go back so much it hurts.

One thing's for sure. If I don't do something soon, I'll get stuck here forever. There'll always be another car to clean. Like the thoughts going round and round inside my head, it's an unending cycle.

Other people's shoes

I take a job working as a Community Service Volunteer for the local council. My job is to apply Community Service Court Orders to juvenile delinquents. It's a pilot scheme to see if teenage offenders can do community work instead of being sent to jail. My brief is to inspire them with a sense of responsibility by doing good deeds for others. I'm paid a trainee's subsistence wage – fourteen pounds a week and the rent on my dad's bedsit.

I find projects for the offenders. Decorating old people's houses, removing junk like shopping trolleys and old tyres from the local river, clearing piles of earth and washing mediaeval pottery shards on archaeological digs with the Kingston Museum.

And when I'm not doing that, I learn what it would be like to become a full-time community worker. I work with patients in a mental hospital, learn the ropes shadowing social workers and help on the community gardens.

There's one episode that sticks in my mind: my first day in the local mental hospital. Brenda, a staff sister doing her rounds, offers me a guided tour. We cross the grounds where men and women are drifting around, directionless. Some are dressed, others undressed, their trousers, skirts and underwear left lying around on the grass. Brenda doesn't give them a second glance. When I ask she explains that they're the ones who don't cause a fuss so they're left to their own devices.

We walk through endless corridors where line after line of patients sit at tables weaving rubbish bins out of basketwork. In the psychiatric ward, others sit around chain smoking and playing card games of their own invention. Finally we go upstairs into what Brenda calls the 'vegetable wards'. Rows of beds line the walls. Light streams in from tall Victorian windows. Everything's in order, crisp and clean, except for the patients, who are strapped to their beds. Some in straight jackets, others catatonic, with drips feeding and draining them. Brenda's been working here for so long she's become hardened to their condition. You'd have to be to work here.

Some pull at their restraints, some nod or rock back and forth, one shakes like a jelly, others whine and slobber.

We stop at one poor man, crunched up like a cockroach stranded on its back and Brenda explains, "Kenneth here is our longest resident, twenty three years I believe, though I've only been here sixteen myself. He hasn't made a noise in all that time. We feed him through that drip there."

I feel the horror of Kenneth's circumstance. Brenda is so matter of fact about him, without a shred of sympathy. I can't help but put myself in his place, wondering what it must be like to be Kenneth in a body without a mind or worse, misdiagnosed. What if he's all there inside? Thinking, feeling and living, just not able to communicate with the outside world?

There's no way I can work here without blocking out my feelings like Brenda has long ago – and that means becoming closed to life. As we pass through ward after ward of the most awful possibilities for humanity I'm left speechless. I'm holding back tears and she can see I'm upset.

"Don't worry dear. They don't know where they are you know. They're off somewhere else, I don't know where. Promise. Lots of people get a bit affected when they first start here but you soon get used to it. Just remember they're not really here."

I hope she's right, but how can she know?

"I'm sorry, I just can't believe what sort of life these people have."

"We do what we can, which isn't very much. As long as they're warm and clean and fed, that's about all we can do. They're here for life and sometimes, I think we are too."

I imagine myself in Kenneth's shoes. It isn't so far-fetched. My brain had been starved of oxygen for over nine minutes. I could have woken up like Kenneth.

*

The volunteer job comes to an end, the pilot scheme gets the funding for a professional graduate to take over, and I get a job as a manager for a housing association in Notting Hill. The government gives us grants to renovate dilapidated houses in order to provide homes for ex-drug addicts, thieves and psychiatric patients. It provides us with housing too: communal living with eight or ten like-minded people and one or two referrals. I manage the houses in Notting Hill, renovating and repairing, mediating in disputes, organising parties and fund raisers, buying whole-foods in bulk from suppliers, distributing it at cost to the residents, doing the books and chasing up back rent.

On top of this job, in the summers I become an adventure playground leader in an inner-city community garden. It's a time of optimism and I'm caught up in it. The ideals of the Windsor Free Festival are still alive somewhere: a new model for inner-city living based on cooperation, sharing and mutual support. The things I'd learnt in the Light are the most important.

*

What was I thinking? I must've been crazy. By the time I'm twenty-one I'm disillusioned with it all. I've had it with trying to help others.

First off, in the mental hospital the line between staff and patients becomes fuzzy, then blurry, and then it disappears altogether. They behave as madly as each other. I guess over time the staff discover that's the best way to control the patients, but after a few weeks I can't tell them apart. It looks like the inmates are running the asylum.

In Social Services, professional carers care more about their jobs than about caring. It seems to me that half of them are in greater need of social work than their clients. From the sidelines, I learn all about office politics, pecking orders, the flexing of egos, backbiting, rumour mongering and petty squabbles over status. It had only been a year since I'd left Kingston Grammar and I'd found myself back in the school playground.

As for the young offenders, they couldn't believe their luck. The courts had let them back on the streets. As far as they were concerned, the jobs I invented for them were a scam and they had a much better time of it than me. They were in a gang and I was the enemy.

And the ideals of communal housing? Those of us in charge have the naïve idea that societies can be changed for the better from the grassroots up. Our optimism blinds us. The thieves, drug addicts and psychiatric patients cause havoc with the experiment. It only takes one thief to undermine a whole house of idealists, no matter how good their intentions. Things go missing, cash, jewellery. Everyone suspects, but nobody wants to accuse. The same goes in different ways for the psychiatric patients and drug addicts. One depressed person sulking in the kitchen all day can bring a whole house down. One junkie's syringe in the bathroom can risk a kid's safety.

Meanwhile, the adventure playground in Paddington is split between the Caribbean gangs and the West London Skinheads. I spend most of my time breaking up fights.

Doing the right thing simply isn't as easy as I'd first thought. It's only taken me a couple of years of working in the community to become a cynic. I make a decision: It isn't for me. It's not my place to help other people. Who am I to think I have something to offer? On a philosophical level, I'm not even sure if anyone can ever really help anyone else. According to the Light Beings, we all have our own potentials to realise.

I decide that people are responsible for themselves. It's the environment that needs looking after. In future that's what I'll focus on, especially seeing as it was my love of Nature that saved me from the demonic humans. But that's not going to happen overnight. I need money to live.

Jobs are still hard to come by and in the dole office I'm offered the chance of starting an apprenticeship. The choices are: two years to become a plumber, electrician or bricklayer; or two weeks of driving lessons to become a truck driver. I become a truck driver.

It's an odd choice but it has its attractions. Getting away from people is one of them. Then there's the freedom of the road and no boss looking over my shoulder. My only contact with base is to call in from a public phone box every so often. I work as an agency driver taking loads whenever and wherever I choose, starting on three axles and working up to articulated trucks. I drive loads back and forth to Germany, Austria and Italy. White goods and machine tools there, machine tools and white goods back. It seems to me a pointless exchange but no doubt there's a profit in it for someone.

My work is the exact opposite of everything I believe in: the lessons from the Light and the ideals of Windsor Common. I am a tiny cog in the wheels of commerce driving a dirty truck and polluting the environment with diesel fumes. How did my life turn out like this?

I can see the sequence of events unfolding over the last three years, starting with my parents blocking my ambitions to go to art college, following on to panic attacks in university lecture theatres, to dropping out and washing cars, to social work and social housing, to here. Each chapter moving further away from what I wanted. It all makes sense. I can see how I've arrived here. What I can't see, what I won't let myself see for the sake of my own sanity, is how it all started unravelling with my beyond-death experience.

On the road, I live by myself in my cab. Long hauls down motorways give me time to think. I cross paths with other drivers and find camaraderie on the road. I enjoy these encounters and pick up tips about the best truck stops; where the food is good and you won't get any hassle.

Driving empty motorways in first light, looking forward to the sun rising over the horizon, always travelling, never arriving. I could be the only person on the planet. I'm on the fringes of society, crossing empty landscapes, bypassing urban centres, lost in my own wilderness. I find it comforting.

At night I park up on lifeless industrial estates alongside warehouses the size of ocean liners, looming out of the darkness in pools of sodium light. These places are weirdly post-apocalyptic. I lock the doors and bury myself in a duvet high inside the cab of my Scania. I'm cushioned in a fold-down bed, twelve feet above the ground, the heating turned up against ice coating the windscreen. Safe and warm in a cocoon. I work on my map and read books about philosophy, still trying to find the rational explanations I need for the metaphysical universe. I make notes in the margins into the early hours of the morning. I'm strangely happy in a foreign country where I don't speak the language, as alone as I was in the grey mist. A long haul from anyone I can call a friend, I enjoy my solitude. Sink or swim, it makes me stronger.

On the road

I pick up hitchhikers waiting on slip roads out of motorway services. Swedish, French, Italians and Germans. Mostly, we speak in broken English, though I can muddle through a conversation in French. I listen to their stories, about where they're going and where they've been. People open up to me. I reckon it's because we're strangers who will never meet again, or something to do with the fact I'm listening to them but not looking at them, keeping my eyes on the road. Or else it's the hypnotic effect of mile after mile of endless tarmac.

My passengers are hitching lifts in search of work, or to a holiday or to reconnect with friends and lovers. Whichever it is, one way or another they're all following their own paths. It makes me wonder where I'm going. After all, I'm the driver with the destination and they're the hitchhikers. But it dawns on me that they know where their hearts are leading them and I don't.

When there aren't any hitchhikers and I'm alone in my cab, I follow the arguments of philosophy like a road map through the centuries. Some philosophers take detours away from the big issues of existence and get diverted by the affairs of mankind, but there are a few in every generation who stay on track, asking the same deep questions I'm asking myself:

Who are we? Seeing as my consciousness continued after my heart stopped, how could I exist as a mind detached from its body?

Where are we? Where is the Light, the Dark, what's in-between? If the earth is so solid, then where did all the stuff go when I left my body? What happened to time and space?

Books about philosophy are dense. I get lost trying to follow the arguments. There are too many Greeks with long names. The closer I get to a solution, the further away it seems to move. It keeps me awake at night and when at last I fall asleep it inhabits my dreams. By day, tracing the white lines on the road, I zone out at the wheel talking to imaginary friends. The first to turn up is the father of rationalism.

"Nothing is real. Everything is an illusion of your senses."

"Really? Seeing as we're hurtling down the autobahn at eighty miles an hour, forty-tons at our backs, I'd like to be sure of that before I crash."

"The only thing you can be sure of is your reason, and my reason tells me that what my senses perceive is an illusion. They can't be trusted."

"Why not?"

"Why *not*?" Parmenides can't believe my ignorance and thinks me stupid. "Because your senses lie. When I dream I think my dream is real but when I wake I know I was dreaming. See? The same is true of when I am awake. It is simply another dream."

"But what about my experience? That was more real than any dream, and yet I wasn't asleep. I was brain-dead. However solid it appears, this physical reality has a transient, fleeting quality compared to existence in the Light."

"Exactly. Look around you. Appearances are transitory. The scenery passes and then it's gone. This cab is a bubble. This windscreen is like the lens in your eye. Inside the bubble is reality and outside is an illusion. See that forest? Now it is gone. See those vineyards? Now they are gone. There is only one road to follow and on that road are many signs that point to the same conclusion. Our senses lie."

"Is that why they call you the father of rationalism?"

"Do they?" He looks pleased with himself, "Tell me more."

"Well you're supposed to be one of the first dualists."

"*One* of the first?"

"OK. The first. You introduced the idea that your mind is a separate entity from the physical world around you."

"Yes I did, didn't I." He puffs himself up. "We arrive at this conclusion through reason not through the delusions of our senses. The beginning and ending of all things is an illusion because what exists has always existed and must always exist."

"That sounds like Einstein's theory of the mass conservation of energy."

"This theory I do not know. Neither this Einstein, but I know I was the first to think it."

"Einstein said energy can neither be created nor destroyed. So everything that exists has always existed. There can be nothing new, including ourselves?"

"I couldn't have put it better myself."

"That's one of the things I knew to be true in the Light – that we have all existed for a very long time. So what about my experience? What do you have to say about the metaphysical universe?"

"I do not understand what you are talking about."

"OK. Infinity, the void. I entered infinity, a metaphysical world."

"There is no infinity. There is no void. If there were, it would already have to be filled with something, so it can't be empty. The cosmos has a binary structure of fire and aether on one side, and ignorant night on the other. These are wound about each other in variant measures."

"Well, the aether was filled with the wisest and most loving Light and the ignorant night, the darkest evil."

"So it was full already?"

"Yes."

"So it wasn't a void. Was it permanent?"

"Yes. Eternal."

"If that is so, you were outside of the world of illusion, in the realm of reason. That which I named the World of Logos."

"So, let me get this right, according to you, the hospital room that I left behind and everyone in it was an illusion of my senses in the first place."

"Correct. You should know that better than anyone. Think yourself lucky. You've seen the World of Logos."

"Don't listen to him. He's the illusion. He's so full of shit it's bursting out of his arse." A wizened old man in rags, looking like an ancient olive tree is reclining behind us on the bunk bed. He is scruffy and unkempt in comparison to regal, manicured Parmenides.

Parmenides bristles, "Who's that?" and turns up his nose as if there's bad smell.

"Don't pretend you don't know me. It's Heraclitus, and it's your ideas that are the illusion."

"My ideas are the only things that aren't illusions. Why, compared to your nonsensical rants, my ideas are blindingly obvious. What was it you said? 'The river both flows and doesn't flow.' What's that supposed to mean?"

Heraclitus corrects him, "What I said was, 'We both step and do not step in the same rivers. We are and are not.' No doubt too cryptic for you to understand, but I am cryptic because the truth of Nature is wont to hide herself. He who does not expect the unexpected will not find it, since the unexpected is trackless and unexplored."

"I hear you're living the life of a hermit in the wilderness, eating lichens off rocks. No wonder you're so cryptic." Parmenides is getting antsy.

"If you lived more in Nature and less in your city you'd know more of her designs. Wisdom is universal, there for all to see, but many live as if they have a wisdom of their own." Heraclitus has a dig at his rival.

"My wisdom is my own," Parmenides objects, "The passing of the seasons, the tides, the cycle of life and death are all illusions compared to the clarity of my logic."

"Bah!" Heraclitus dismisses him.

"Hang on, you two." I interrupt. "Can we go back to the rivers thing?" Parmenides gathers his robes around him, stares out of the offside window and settles into a sulk while Heraclitus explains.

"The river flows in the same riverbed but we can never put our feet into the same water twice. The water is not the same, and also, we are not the same. Time has changed both us and the water."

I'm excited, "That sounds to me like Einstein's theory of special relativity. We and the water occupy space and the space exists in a fourth dimension, time. We are locked in the space-time continuum. Everything exists in a relative state of perpetual flux and universal transformation."

"I couldn't have put it better myself. Who is this Einstein of whom you speak?"

"You're before his time."

"This idea of flux and flow, is my idea then. Not of this Einstein." And, having had his say, Heraclitus slumps back on my bed.

When I had stepped out of space and time, the way time worked was so clear, but it is so hard to get my head around it since I've been back. There must be some really obvious point I'm missing. Something about the split between space and time – how the split is actually the thing that creates this world and how we couldn't exist without it. If only I could remember, I feel sure I can solve the problem of what happened to all the stuff when I left the hospital room. Frustrating is not the word for it, I'm beating myself up trying to remember what the Light Beings told me I would have to forget.

Heraclitus coughs to get my attention and points a finger at Parmenides, "He says the world is permanent, nothing ever changes. Bah! I say everything changes, everything flows and nothing ever stands still. The road up and the road down are one and the same. In the circumference of the circle the beginning and the end are common. Out of discord comes the fairest harmony."

I interrupt, "So our senses aren't an illusion."

"Of course not. If we crash this truck, will not forty tons propel itself though our bodies? Will it not hurt and then we die?"

I have to agree.

"Nature is made of opposites: hot and cold, light and dark, male and female, good and bad." Heraclitus is on a roll, "But opposites are the same: hot and cold are born of heat; light and dark, degrees of shade; male and female, different sexes; and good and bad, just different intentions and consequences of our actions."

Parmenides has been paying attention, waiting for his break. "A gloomy thought from one who hates humankind," he says jadedly. "According to him, we are all caught up in the ebb and flow of life and we have no free will over our destinies."

Heraclitus snaps back, "We have every control over our destiny if only we could see it. Our character creates our destiny. It shapes our fate. But we cannot know it. We are too simple and life is too short to see its workings. Existence is so complex that even sleepers are workers and collaborators in what goes on in the universe.

"Life is nothing more than a child at play, moving pieces in a game. The whole of history is merely a child building a sandcastle by the sea. That child is the whole majesty of man's power in the world."

"Oh don't listen to him, he's not called the weeping philosopher for nothing," exclaims Parmenides.

Heraclitus counters, "If you saw the things I've seen, you'd be melancholic too."

"So what about my experience." I ask.

"What of it?" asks Heraclitus.

"Is there room for the metaphysical in your physics?"

"Everything in this world is physical. The things that can be seen, heard and learned are what I prize most."

"Then you prize illusions above everything," Parmenides taunts him. Heraclitus won't be drawn. He shakes his head in exasperation, "Of this metaphysics of which you speak, I know nothing. This universe, which is the same for all, has not been made by any god or man, but it always has been, is, and will be, an ever-living fire, kindling itself and going out by regular measures. All I know is this: Everything is one."

This I too learnt in the Light, as certain as anything. It's probably the Light's greatest lesson. However, what I learn from my books is that there's a fault line that creates a rift between the philosophers, even today, and Parmenides and Heraclitus stand on either side of it.

The fault line describes opposite interpretations of mind and matter. On his side of the rift, Heraclitus's point of view is monist — only the physical world exists. On the other side, Parmenides' view is dualist — the mind interacts with the brain, but fundamentally they are made of different substances. Parmenides isn't only a dualist, he's also an idealist, one step further removed from the monist viewpoint. He thinks consciousness is the only thing that is real and the entire physical world is an illusion.

It's clear which side of the fault line I'm standing on. My consciousness left a brain-dead body, so I have to be a dualist. Am I an idealist as well? I'm not sure. Is the entire physical world an illusion? It was from the perspective of the Light. And when I returned that sense of illusion remained which places me in the idealist camp. However, the longer I'm here and the further I'm distanced from my experience, the more solid the physical world becomes.

What occurs to me is how firmly my feet had been planted on the monist side of the rift before my beyond-death experience. How certain I had been in the solidity of the world and that science would solve all the mysteries of birth, life and death, probably in my lifetime. And how uncertain of this I am now.

*

I've past Pforzheim without noticing. I've been carried away by the philosophers' arguments. I need to turn off Autobahn 8 and find the slip road to my next drop in Stuttgart. I leave my imaginary conversations behind and return to the present to find my direction when something bursts open in my mind like a breaking dam: Heraclitus's description of the flow of the river through time, Einstein's space-time continuum, Parmenides illusion of the senses, it all comes together and unblocks a stream of thought.

Where had all the 'stuff' gone when I died? Parmenides says it disappeared when my physical senses stopped functioning, as all the stuff in the world is simply an illusion of the senses. Heraclitus says it disappeared because it was all intrinsically linked to my own position in the stuff as an observer in time. Time and place are co-dependent.

In my two life reviews – first in the void on my way to the Light, and second with the Light Beings – both times there were screens with scenes projected on them like in a film but in 3D, like one of those laser holograms they've just invented. And I was physically inside each scene. Every moment of my life was actually, physically, locked into a slice of time, like a thin sheet of Perspex, and I could revisit each one as if turning the pages of a book.

Here, in this world, we inhabit the space-time continuum. Time is the fourth dimension of our three-dimensional world but it's disconnected from the other three. At least that's how we perceive it. But in the other world, time behaved differently. It was both present and eternal. I could perceive all times, locked into slices of four-dimensional holograms, at any time, while I can only perceive three dimensions in this physical world. Height, breadth, depth. That's all we can see. The past and the future aren't visible like they were in the other world.

In this life, time has only one face: the present. And if I try and stop the clock and locate the present it's already flown by.

I remember something Einstein said that hadn't made much sense before, but now it's a catalyst. "Time only exists so that everything in space doesn't happen all at once." The meaning of a space-time continuum becomes tangible. Space can't exist without a time to exist in and time needs space to fill it.

The hospital ward and all the stuff disappeared when the energy needed to keep my etheric self tied to my physical body in the space-time continuum ran out. My energy had only a limited amount of time it could stay connected to the physical world, a world that could no longer support it and to which it no longer belonged, and when it had run out of energy to remain moving with the sweep of time, I got left behind in the mist.

Time is the crest of a tsunami carrying all the artefacts of space along with it – buildings, trees, cars, people – in a rush from out of the past into the future. There is actually no past nor future, these are just our subjective perceptions, the way we like to see things. In the space-time continuum the tsunami is rolling through eternal, 'all-at-once time' in a constant present and that's all we can see.

Everybody is surfing that wave until they wipe out. I fell off the board – I wiped out. The wave left me behind tumbling through the backwash, in all-at-once time. All the stuff didn't disappear, it simply moved on in the present.

A-toma

In a warehouse in Stuttgart, I'm waiting for German muscle to unload my machine tools, arguing with myself about the rift between the philosophers. I must be an idealist as that's what I learnt in the Light but the more I study, the more I realise that as far as modern thinking goes, I'm standing on the wrong side of the divide.

I'm pondering where I fit in when another philosopher arrives in my head. It's Democritus, the father of the atom and he's chuckling to himself.

"What's so funny?" I ask.

"Those two old philosophers, they'll never stop arguing even though they're both right in their own way."

"Are they?"

"They're two sides of the same coin. One says everything is permanent the other, everything changes. Well, I united both sides."

"How did you do that?"

He's boastful, like the others. "By discovering that the things that are permanent also cause everything else to change. It was me who discovered a-toma, the un-cuttable building blocks of nature."

"I thought it was your teacher, Leucippus, who came up with that idea."

He smarts, "Well. I suppose you could say that, but it was me who put the work in. I applied atoms to everything."

"To everything?" I'm thinking of consciousness.

"Everything. Water atoms are soft and pliable, fire atoms tiny and spherical, capable of penetrating solid bodies. Air atoms are whirly and light and iron atoms, solid and strong with hooks that lock them together."

"OK. And…?"

"As for taste, small pointy atoms taste sharp, like salt, large round atoms, sweet. They are all indestructible. This I proved."

"What about our minds? Are our minds indestructible?"

"The mind is made of soul atoms inside the brain that are small and spherical like fire atoms. When we die, they scatter into thin air and reassemble..." He gestures lazily.

"...But they don't take us along with them." I interrupt. This is where I'd started out four years ago. "What about my experience?"

"Whether soul atoms or rock atoms, all atoms are lifeless."

"So we are lifeless. Simple machines at the beck and call of our mechanics?"

"No, *we* are not lifeless. Our soul atoms power and motivate our bodies."

"So our soul atoms are not lifeless."

Democritus looks perplexed, "Of this I am not sure. I have not considered this in enough detail. But I am convinced life is mechanical. What do your quantum physicists think?"

"You've heard of quantum physics?"

"I try and keep up. I believe your new science of quantum mechanics might hold the key to your questions."

Quantum mechanics? The thought's popped into my head out of nowhere. Out of an imaginary conversation with a philosopher long dead but who still has more to say, "Perhaps you fell into the void; into the space between the atoms." He proffers.

Could that have happened? It hasn't occurred to me. All along I've been assuming my etheric body was the same size and shape as my physical body. That's what it had felt like. But senses are deceptive and outside of the world of stuff, size is irrelevant. It was impossible to judge space or size in the grey mist. It was all the same. In that vast emptiness I could've been less than the size a full stop. I'm going to have to take a massive jump in scale from the macro to the micro but I sense that's where I'm heading, into the space between the atoms.

*

By the time I reach Munich and park up for the night, it feels like my cab is bursting at the seams with philosophers.

"There are three souls that I can divine; the vegetative, the sensitive and the rational. Only humans have all three," announces Aristotle.

"Our souls are transformed into the Seminal Reason of the Universe by the artistic Fire of Nature," says Zeno.

"Death is nothing to worry about because as long as we exist, death is not there and when death comes, we no longer exist," says Epicurus, stoically.

"There is no difference between life and death so I might as well be alive as dead," Diogenes declares, cynically.

I chase the philosophers out of my head and look at what I've discovered for my map.

I draw a picture of the universe supported on a scaffolding of spheres. On the outside I place Pythagoras's Creative Fire with the current of Cosmic Breath, flowing through the holes of the stars. It's not right. I don't need his geography. I need a metaphysical location. I rip it up.

I draw Xenophanes' universal force of everything - matter and energy – embracing all things. It's a sphere. It can stand in for other abstract ideas like Aristotle's the Unmoved Mover or Heraclitus's Creative Fire or Zeno's the Artistic Creator. But it doesn't relate to anything I can call a map. I rip it up.

Next is Plato. His account of Er's journey is the closest description to my own journey that I've come across. I keep it. And as for Parmenides; like Plato, he reasoned that everything is an illusion except for the world of Logos, Plato's world of pure Ideas. That's where I went. But where is it?

In the opposite camp, the monists or materialists deduced that nothing exists except for physical mechanisms, so consciousness somehow has to be reduced to a function of the brain. If Democritus is right and everything is made of lifeless atoms then there's no room for my experience. It can't exist in a material world.

I hit a wall. The monist perspective is our world-view. For two thousand years philosophers and scientists from Aristotle to Newton have been dismantling the cogs and wheels they thought made the universe turn. If they are right, and existence is reducible to the sum of its parts – if we are fuelled by chemical reactions alone and consciousness is nothing more than the flow of electromagnetic energy through our synapses – then my experience is impossible.

And that's the thing. Despite everything I've been though I'm still a confirmed empiricist. I broke though the membrane between this world and the next but I haven't a clue how to prove it. As my father drilled into me, anything that can't be proved by many observers repeating the same experiment and producing the same results simply doesn't exist. I'm sitting on a bench with only Pythagoras and Plato for company and they're over two and a half thousand years old.

I'm fighting against the current, struggling to stay afloat. Science's world-view is the exact opposite of my search. I don't fit in. According to the materialists, the route I traveled isn't on the map. But I know it is. It has to be.

Seeking Nirvana

I've travelled as far as I can with the philosophers and reached a divide I cannot bridge. Where to look next? I'm drawn to Buddhism. It looks less like a religion and more like a step-by-step guidebook to enlightenment. Locked in the desperate struggle with the demonic humans, the thought had crossed my mind to ask for help from the Buddha. But I couldn't do it. My fight had demanded the utmost integrity and, truthfully, I'd known I wasn't a practising Buddhist. I'd only ever bought a poster of a mandala and read a few books. I was a tourist.

I can get by working a couple of weeks a month so in between jobs from the trucking agency I start to look at Buddhism more deeply. I discover that the earliest Buddhists were probably the first to study consciousness, the very thing I'm desperate to understand. They arrived at a distinction between the consciousness we experience in everyday life and an ultimate ground state of consciousness that is radiant and clear. They observed that our everyday state of mind comes out of second-by-second reactions to the input of our senses, which are filtered through the personalities we have accumulated over many years.

The ultimate ground state of consciousness only emerges on the point of death. It is a natural unencumbered stream of consciousness that carries us on from one lifetime to the next. The first Buddhists believed that by calming the involuntary activity of the mind through meditation it's possible to experience this primordial consciousness while still on this earth.

Seeing as my search is a quest to understand how my consciousness could exist outside of my body, maybe it's time I became a Buddhist?

A friend of mine, Richard, has the same idea. He's been studying Buddhism in a monastery just outside London and he thinks he's ready to go on retreat. He's seeking enlightenment and when I ask, he explains, "Buddhists say that when you isolate yourself from the distractions of the outside world and the desires of your ego, your mind quietens. You become aware that all of your desires and delusions are distractions of the senses. Buddhism teaches that it's possible to turn off your desires and blow them out like the flame of a candle. Nirvana is the stillness of mind that remains."

I'm reminded of Parmenides and Plato; their idea that the physical world is merely an illusion of the senses, how only the rational mind can perceive reality.

The monastery follows two paths: silence, to calm the mind; and chanting, to cancel out distractions by chanting repetitive mantras. I wonder if this might be what I'm searching for – a path back into the peace of mind I experienced in the Light. Richard has signed up for a month's retreat and I agree to join him.

The idea of not talking for a month is daunting but I figure it's not that different to the endless hours I've spent on the road, day and night, talking to myself. However, this isn't the only thing making me uneasy; there's something else I can't quite put my finger on.

I sign up anyway, take a break from work, quit smoking and drinking and arrive feeling refreshed. The first thing the monks do is split Richard and me into different dormitories. Junior monks lead me into the kitchen and assign me tasks. They don't talk, they just demonstrate what I have to do.

It's all a bit weird. In my search for enlightenment I didn't expect to find myself washing-up for over forty people, sweeping floors, then carrying out rubbish, but I understand these menial tasks are all part of the process of giving up my ego.

I try to follow the ritualistic blessings at mealtimes. I sit at the back of the temple behind the junior monks and higher initiates while a priest incants the liturgies at prayer times. All without understanding a word.

Through the first week and the start of the second I fight negative states of mind: boredom from the dullness of the routine, annoyance at the pecking order, hunger from the bland diet, aching tiredness from rising at four o'clock in the morning and anger with myself for all these thoughts when I'm supposed to be quietening my mind. More than anything else I'm unwilling to let go of my ego. The more I try, the more I rebel. Something is stopping me. I know it's a copout, but on the eleventh day, I quit.

The monks say nothing as I bow my goodbyes. I see complete understanding in their faces but I feel like a failure. The first newsagents I pass, I buy a pack of cigarettes and matches and stand outside inhaling deeply.

I make excuses. I tell myself that becoming a monk is running away from life's possibilities. There are too many things I haven't done, and there's an urgency to life I can't shake off. I'm twenty-one and feel like everything is waiting to happen but nothing's started yet.

In the monastery there were too many thoughts getting in the way for me to free my mind and if I couldn't free it then and there, where could I? I don't want to admit it, but many of the thoughts distracting me weren't mine. They were my father's – things he'd drummed into me, what he wants from me – to become a success in his eyes and not the failure that is all he can see.

Putting that to one side, there are other reasons why I couldn't let go of my ego. The fact is, I'm scared of relinquishing my identity. But surely anxiety about losing my identity doesn't make sense: I've already experienced what that feels like. Shaking off all the layers of self that I'd accumulated in my lifetime, like the layers of an onion, was a necessary step to passing through the doorway into the Light. All that was left was a name that no longer belonged to me and I'd shrugged that off too.

So why should I feel anxious now? Isn't this what I crave? To get closer to the state I was in inside the Light. Or was losing my ego actually a traumatic experience? Seventeen years spent constructing my identity and when I relinquished it, I was left only with the knowledge of how flimsy and insubstantial it all is. The scaffolding we build for ourselves is rickety, it has no foundation and it's so easily demolished.

Is that why I felt like an alien when I came back to earth? Or why, finding myself surrounded by crowds in the high street, I'd felt as fragile as a moth? Or why I suffered panic attacks in the lecture theatre packed full of other students?

I can see a pattern again. I suppose it can't be healthy in this life to abandon your identity all in one go as I'd been forced to, flying towards the doorway of Light. There are reasons we all spend years insulating ourselves from each other in the first place: survival. Some people grow thicker and thicker layers of shell simply to stop others getting through. I'm trying to do the opposite: to remain open.

So far, approaching life with an empathic attitude towards others hasn't done me much good. Trying to put myself in other people's shoes doesn't mean they're trying to put themselves in mine. In a crowd I'm not as shielded against the rest of humanity as I need to be without the armour everyone carries around with them. Maybe my beyond-death experience has left me vulnerable in ways I haven't taken on board. Wounds remain open that I need to close.

That must be why I didn't want to relinquish control to the hierarchy of monks in the monastery. Once was already one time too many. With the monastic life off the table, I buy a translation of The Tibetan Book of the Dead and conscientiously set about studying. It's the Buddhist manual for the dying: hundreds of pages of incantations to be chanted as death approaches to ease the soul into the after-death plane. Could the Book of the Dead be my route map into the afterlife?

When the five lights of brilliant wisdom dawn, fearless, bravely, may I know them as myself! When the forms of the Lords mild and fierce arise, bold and fearless, may I recognise the between! Now when I suffer by the power of negative evolution, may the Archetype Deities dispel that suffering! When reality crashes with a thousand thunders may they all become OM MANI PADME HUM!

I study page after page. I can understand bits here and there but it doesn't speak to me. It's written for eighth century Tibetan monks with a life of Buddhist teachings behind them, not for a twentieth-century grammar school boy from Kingston-upon-Thames. I toy with the idea of a pilgrimage to Nepal; it's fashionable in the counter culture. An overland bus, a right of passage, as if this will bring me closer to enlightenment. Forget it, it's not for me. I can change my geography but I can't change my skin. My beyond-death experience was unique to me, an atheist schoolboy from English suburbia. It hadn't been a Buddhist afterlife just as it hadn't been a Christian one.

*

A few weeks later I bump into Richard in the pub. He didn't last the course either.

"So did you find Nirvana?"

Richard chuckles, "No, it's the search of a lifetime and in the monastery I failed spectacularly. I blew it. But you would have too."

There was a beautiful girl in the group and from the start they were attracted to each other.

"We tried to ignore it, like we were both there for the best reasons and the last thing I wanted to do was to distract her, but..." Richard shrugs.

They were there to free themselves of their physical desires but their desires won. While keeping their vows of silence they stole moments in hidden corners in the monastery, "It was so sexy..." Richard grins. They left the retreat after a few weeks and jumped into bed. "It was fantastic while it lasted, even if it only lasted a few days. All that build-up. Fantasising about what we'd be like together with no talk getting in the way of our imaginations. When we finally started talking there was nothing there. We had nothing in common."

Richard might be annoyed with himself but I'm envious. It doesn't sound like a waste of time to me. Maybe the sex was what he'd been searching for. He says "Well one thing it taught me was to stop putting women on a pedestal," which makes me think of Jenny and how I've done the same.

While I commiserate with Richard I'm thinking more about Jenny than about him. I've made her into the perfect model, an object of my romantic love, and I've forgotten she's made of flesh and blood. I'm still kicking myself about missing my chance with her in Kew Gardens. It's not just my loyalty to Nick that I blame, but also going to a boys-only grammar school. Opportunities to practise with girls, like meeting up in the Jolly Brewers, were thin on the ground. The school system separates us just when we should be learning how to get on with each other. I wonder if Jenny is still with Nick and if she isn't, is she still into me?

The Jolly Brewers

Standing at the bar in the Jolly Brewers, everything and nothing has changed. It still stinks of beer-soaked carpet and old ashtrays, under-aged drinkers still huddle in their own cliques, and music still drowns out conversation.

But now everything is punk. Sham 69 and The Clash blare from the speakers, the new look is spiky hair, dog collars, ripped T-shirts, skinny black jeans and safety pin earrings. I'm not one of them and there's an ugly vibe directed my way. If I wasn't built from driving trucks they'd probably close in and pick a fight. But I can see where they're coming from. Punk is nihilist and anarchic, a reflection of a time of recession and unemployment. They've no hope for the future aside from stacking shelves in a supermarket or working on a factory assembly line.

All my old friends have moved on except for one; a drummer called Dave. He's still propping up the bar but he's now sporting a Ramones T-shirt and a stubbly Mohican. He's adapted to the times. Dave was always on the fringes of our gang, never part of it, a loner and a bit of a letch, but I'm glad to see a face I recognise in a pub full of hostility. We talk about old bands we used to play in. It sounds like he's the only musician to have made the crossover into punk while all the rest have given up in disgust at the new wave. Eventually, I slip in the question that's really on my mind.

"You seen Jenny?"
"Yeah. You bet."
"Is she still with Nick?"
"Yeah, if you can call it that."
I don't get it so ask him, "How is she?"
He looks incredulous as if I'm supposed to know.
"She's on top form." Dave takes a slug on his pint and gives me a lecherous grin, "You ever go there?"
"No. Did you?"

"Yeah, you bet!" He smirks, enjoying his moment of one-upmanship, chuffed he has something to boast about. "She's had all of us. Ticking us off her list one by one."

I see red and want to punch his smug face, but I stop and consider what's making me feel this way. Envy that he's been with her? Sticking up for my best mate when really I'm hoping they're not together anymore? Or a sense of virtue that Jenny needs defending from a slight on her character?

Dave's knocked her off the pedestal I've built for her. That's it. And all he's doing is boasting about another of his conquests.

"All of us?" I try not to appear shocked.

"Well not all of us, obviously, I mean not you for starters." There's the urge again to punch his lights out. He names several of our friends and adds, "And who knows who else we don't know about. She's got a reputation around here, that's for sure."

"A reputation?"

"For screwing around. Love'em and leave'em."

"You're kidding?" That doesn't sound like Jenny.

"Really. We couldn't believe it either."

Dave might be a letch but he isn't a liar.

"And Nick?"

"Nick hasn't a clue and no one wants to burst his bubble."

As he talks I don't feel the same about Jenny I did a minute ago, a month ago, a year ago, four years ago in the grey mist. The girl I've idolised all this time has disappeared. She isn't there anymore.

"So what's been going on?"

He doesn't need the prompt. "None of us were talking about it. She got us to promise to keep schtum. I thought she'd leave Nick and go out with me, and it turns out we all thought the same but she was just playing around. When we got to talk about it, y'know, when we clocked her score, we couldn't believe it. I tell you. She's good at covering her tracks."

I'm having difficulty taking all this in. Then I think of Kew Gardens.

"So what's with her?"

"We all like her. I mean not just in that way. She's a cool chick. But she's a heartbreaker."

She was the most beautiful girl in the Jolly Brewers, the object of my unrequited love and the last attachment that kept me arrested in the grey mist. It's only now I can see it for what it is, a romantic illusion. An illusion because I just assumed love went hand in hand with fidelity. How stupid of me.

What I'm learning about the way of the world is that I'm carrying around a conscience that, as far as I can tell, has no useful purpose in this life. And as far as Jenny's concerned, it's only me who's responsible for my delusion. Jenny's never made herself out to be anything different to who she is – flirting with me in the bar, wanting me to seduce her in Kew Gardens – simply practising with boys the same way we practise with girls.

Dave gives me Nick and Jenny's address, a flat in the centre of Kingston above a hardware store. I go round and ring the doorbell. Jenny answers the door. Gone are the loons, beads and hippie chic. She's cropped her hair and is wearing kohl eye shadow and a Clash T-shirt.

"Hello! What on earth are you doing here?"

I've forgotten it's been four years. "That's a nice welcome."

"So? What are you doing here?"

"Well it's good to see you too."

Jenny composes herself, "Yeah it's good to see you. I guess. How are you?"

"I'm good. Is Nick there? You going to invite me in?" I've put her on a spot. Didn't mean to.

"OK. Why don't you come in?"

Upstairs, Nick's making dinner. He's as surprised as Jenny to see me. All three of us feel awkward. We don't hug or slap each other on the back. Time has passed and we're not the same as we were. We're uncomfortable with the people we used to be, the friendships we've left behind. We slip into small talk, trying to find our feet. I wish I'd phoned first but I explain that I didn't have a number.

Jenny is on edge. I reckon she realises I know about her affairs and she's scared I'll say something to Nick. She bridges the gaps between our lines of conversation, keeping us on track in case I switch points and derail her life. There's no opportunity in their one-bed flat to pull Jenny to one side and have a word, but what's it got to do with me anyway?

Instinctively I feel I should say something to Nick, but who am I kidding? I didn't tell him about Kew Gardens. I want to help my mate but neither of them is going to thank me for destroying their relationship. And what right have I to interfere? Who gave me the right to judge? I don't even know what the 'right thing' is anymore.

In the Light it was all so simple. There were no secrets as there were no illusions. The Light Beings didn't judge me so I'm not going to judge Jenny.

The three of us share a beer and catch up on where we've been and what we've been up to and I leave before they eat, turning down an invitation to stay for dinner.

Samsara

While I've been driving trucks across Europe, friends from the Housing Association have rented a house in Portobello Road. They offer me the attic. They've left the communal housing to the mental patients, thieves and junkies from the council for the sake of their own peace of mind.

I share the attic rooms with Marie who teaches yoga when she's not trading jewellery in India. She has a yoga studio next to her bedroom and I have an art studio next to mine. I paint bad oils and watercolours without any technique: banks of cumulonimbus clouds, white doorways against black backgrounds, ghostly cities, golden volcanic rivers and bubbling black canvases of tar. I am obsessed, with neither the talent nor education to make anything good.

Marie is older and I reckon a lot wiser than me. I like her. She has a slim body that hides strength and flexibility from her yoga practice. Her impish face gives her a look much younger than her years. Maybe her face set in this mischievous expression when she was just a kid but it suits her. She laughs at life and teases me for taking things so seriously. She ribs me about my paintings but there's a deeper side to her. One night we're alone, sharing a bottle of red wine, and I decide to let her in on what I'm trying to paint and why.

First I tell her about the beyond-death experience. I think about leaving out the demonic humans, like when I told my father. Putting myself in Marie's shoes, I figure she won't want to know about that place in case it plays on her mind as it does on mine. But Marie is different. When I hesitate she clocks it and demands to know everything, so I tell her everything. She listens. Really listens.

When I've finished telling about the experience, I carry on recounting the effect it's been having on me and finally tackle my dilemmas with Buddhism.

When I get to the end she says, "I always knew there was something weird about you. You're here in this room but you're not really here are you."

"How do you mean?" I ask, thinking I'm as here as anyone else.

"There's a part of you that's always somewhere else. I can feel it. You're in the world but you're not of it. Looking in from a place only you have been."

"Am I?" I ask, self-conscious.

"Don't worry, it's not like anyone else notices. Only me," she jokes. "At first I thought you were a weirdo. Well you are. I mean, a nice weirdo but a weirdo nonetheless. Now I see where you're coming from and I reckon I know someone who can help with your dilemmas."

"You do?" I'm intrigued.

"Yes. Me." Marie laughs. "You've been toying with Buddhism and got nowhere. Well that's no surprise. It's a life's work, sometimes for just one moment of kensho."

"Kensho?"

"A momentary glimpse of enlightenment. Satori is enlightenment, the experience of Nirvana. Kensho is a flicker of satori."

"OK."

"It sounds to me like you're locked in an impossible quandary. You've experienced Nirvana, or at least in the Buddhist understanding, two different levels of Bardo."

"Bardo?"

"Intermediate states between death and rebirth. On a Buddhist map of the afterlife there are thirty-one levels of existence. Four are levels of deprivation, levels of evil below our everyday existence. The rest are levels of Nirvana above our everyday existence. You experienced at least one level of deprivation and then other levels of Nirvana. I'm not surprised you don't know what to do with your experience. And to make things worse, you're disheartened because you've lost your paradise."

I agree.

"Well, I'm not going to suggest you follow the Buddhist path, that's for you to decide. If you do, you might work at it for years and never achieve even one moment of what you've experienced already. You know what? I've spent my life longing for just a glimpse of where you've been. To see what you've seen, it must be…" Marie stops to think, "There aren't words, are there?"

I grin. She gets it. "No. There aren't words."

"I should be envious, but after listening to your story, I'm not. You've experienced both good and evil in Bardo. How do you square that place with this and know what to do with the rest of your life?"

She lets out a long breath, "Phew, that's a hard one."

"Tell me about it."

"You're not doing very well with it are you?"

"Nope." She's right. I'm not.

"That's 'cos you're in your head, not here," she touches her chest. "All this looking for philosophical answers, they're rational answers for your head and you'll never be able to satisfy your head. It's like a hungry monster – the more information you feed it the hungrier it gets."

"I know what you mean."

Marie smiles indulgently and I know she's right. There are many levels of knowledge and the intellect is only one of them. I experienced other ways of knowing in the Light. Absolute knowledge that inhabited my whole being and charged every one of my senses.

"OK. I get it, I'm in my head."

I let Marie continue, "The early Brahminic Yogis adopted yoga as a system of meditation aimed at completely stopping their thoughts, stopping the internal dialogue."

"Internal dialogue?"

"The conversations we all have with ourselves even when we're not talking. Well, in fact, mostly when we're not talking and no one else is around."

"I know what you mean. And it's not just when we're by ourselves. Most people don't listen to what you're saying even when you *are* talking. They're already thinking about what they're going to say next."

"Have you ever wondered who is talking to who when you're on your own?" Marie asks.

"One bit of our mind talking to another bit?"

"Yeah, but who are the characters?" she presses. "Who is the talker and who's the listener?"

"I've never thought about it," thinking of my dialogues with the philosophers on the road.

"Some psychologists say it's a constant dialogue between the adult, the child and the judge or critic, a three-way conversation. That's why it never stops, because it's three-way. There's always someone in the wings waiting for their say."

"Who's the judge, the critic?"

"The adult is your true self, the child is your inner child and the judge is your parents, or an archetype of a parent that might go back for generations."

I remember trying to clear my mind in the Buddhist monastery and finding my father lecturing me, "So my father is inside my head?"

"More than likely and I bet he's a critic."

I think about all the things my father has drummed into me over the years and reluctantly I have to agree. Not only is his voice inside my head, but he doesn't have anything good to say. He's always criticising. I can see how it works.

"Two and a half thousand years ago, Buddhists looked at this constant chatter and called it samsara."

"Samsara?"

"Distractions. Ego. Irrelevance."

"Distractions from what?"

"When you're looking at the world through the characters who talk to you inside your head, you're not seeing it with your own eyes. More than that, you're not seeing it through your heart. Samsara is distraction from being. From what's really going on."

I remember the Light Being's advice, 'Only through the heart can the world be understood.' and ask, "So what happens if you stop your thoughts?"

"You stop the duality between the talker and the listener. You arrive at a singularity. Oneness. Being. Present. Not observing and not observed." Marie smiles and puts her glass down. "If you can achieve that, you're on your way to attaining a supreme state of awareness."

There it is again, the idea of a singularity. Now making its appearance in yoga.

"But when I died my thoughts didn't stop. That's one of the most amazing things about the whole experience. How I was still thinking as myself; observing, having opinions, being able to ask questions."

"I don't know about that," Marie answers. "In the Buddhist way of thinking, souls reincarnate with no memory of their past lives but your life didn't stop. You returned to the same life with all the knowledge of your experience intact, so what happened to you is a mystery. You want to find links between that dimension and this one? Well, I'm offering you a link."

"You are? I don't get it."

"That's cause you're in your head, stupid."

"Oh. Yeah, I forgot."

"The Brahmins who developed yoga had the goal of achieving the non-dual meditative state that happens at death."

"No duality, as in no 'I', no ego, no speaking and listening?"

"Precisely. No watcher and no watched."

"That sounds like what I experienced with the Light Beings, well, what I call the Light Beings. I've no idea who or what they were aside from being a super-consciousness. I know for sure they weren't one of the voices that talk to me inside my head. They had absolute knowledge and absolute wisdom and I was stupid by comparison. The way we communicated was like you described. Conversation happened telepathically and instantaneously. Questions were answered before I'd finished asking. And this state is possible in life?"

"That's what the Brahminic yogis thought. At death they called the state of non-duality, 'Becoming cool' or 'Going out'. They wanted to achieve the same in life. The Buddhists changed it a little as they thought the aim wasn't solely to cease all mental activity. The Buddhist adept, once he's stopped his thoughts, directs his attention at achieving a state of mindful awareness. He focuses on things and, not having any duality of his own, becomes them."

"What? Literally?"

"Who knows? I haven't got there and probably never will."

"Have you stopped your thoughts?"

"...Yes."

"What was it like?"

Marie smiles. "Like not having any thoughts, stupid." She's being facetious, "You think it's something I can describe... in thoughts?" I see her point.

"So when can we start?"

"We can start whenever you want. But clean up your act and stop drinking, OK?"

"OK."

*

It's a hot day in April. Dust motes float through sunbeams in Marie's studio. The calls of market traders ring from the street below. We lay rugs on the painted floorboards, sit cross-legged in loose clothing and I listen to my first lesson.

Marie's approach is neither religious nor spiritual. She teaches yoga the way she's learnt it, as a physical science. She doesn't attach anything in her teaching to any god except for what she calls 'the divine mechanisms within ourselves'.

"The three corner stones of Hatha Yoga are breathing, exercise and meditation. First you have to learn how to breathe."

I think I know how to breathe, but apparently I don't. "Yogis breathe; we pant," explains Marie.

I learn how to breathe from my diaphragm, exhaling twice as long as inhaling, taking a pause between breaths to allow a moment in time for the world to stop. I learn how to stretch and contract muscle groups in the asanas – the exercises – how to slow down and concentrate on each muscle in turn.

The Candle and the Fish, the Plough and the Cobra, the Forward Bend and the Locust, the Bow and the Headstand. Each pair of asanas are dynamic opposites of each other, first stretching one way then the other. The exercises finish with the Spinal Twist to click the vertebra open.

I've become muscle-bound from driving trucks. The asanas demand my muscles move in ways I've never asked them to before. Marie laughs each time I fall off my headstand, "Give it time, you'll get it," she giggles.

And, in between asanas, I learn how to relax in the Corpse Position, lying flat on the carpet, legs together and arms at my side. After breathing and exercises comes meditation.

"The yoga I practise treats the body as a series of muscles and the brain as the biggest muscle of all. So what I want you to do next is turn that brain of yours off," instructs Marie.

I'm ready.

"The brain is the largest and most active muscle in the body. All your thoughts are electro-chemical signals buzzing around between synapses, loads of energy, loads of activity. We're constantly engaged in the internal chattering, the conversation with ourselves that is our default position. We need to shut down that internal dialogue. Start by focussing your attention on one thing only – your breathing."

I concentrate on my breathing, slowly in, twice as slowly out, stopping on each exhalation. Thoughts keep popping into my head. They won't stop.

"My thoughts won't stop," I say.

"And you think it'll happen overnight?" Marie dismisses my impatience.

After a few months' practice I'm getting better at it. Meditation is all about focussing on one thing only – breathing – in order to switch off the rest. Every week, throughout that summer in Portobello Road, we practise together. Marie corrects my postures, "Keep your feet together... push your spine further into the floor... your legs are hanging over your head, make them vertical... I can hear you breathing... relax your neck... rotate slower..." she badgers on.

As July rolls into August, the attic studio gets hotter and hotter. We dispense with loose clothes and practise naked. It's Marie's idea, and for both of us it's entirely nonsexual. The practice is everything. Then one night Marie slips into my bed and without a word, we become lovers.

*

In the autumn, Marie leaves for Nepal to walk her own path. Fiercely concentrating on 'Nothing' in the Corpse Position, I learn how to still my brain.

The sensation is fantastic. Without an 'I' to observe and analyse, my senses expand. When I turn off my internal dialogue, the volume of the world increases; sounds, smells, everything becomes more intense. I can perceive my surroundings simultaneously rather than in a series of thoughts. I am suddenly in the present with no delay between the external world and my internal one.

The stillness is blissful, like floating in a warm calm sea. The boundaries between body and air melt away. The detachment from what I thought of as 'I', as 'myself', reveals another 'self' underlying the first – sensing, observing, experiencing – but somehow standing apart, isolated. I begin to grasp that this 'self' is the one that was left when my heart stopped, the one that travelled into the Light. The core self I didn't know I inhabited.

Lying in the Corpse Position one day, slowly calming my thoughts until they cease, something unexpected happens. My consciousness, as always, stuck inside my head, even when I've stopped my thoughts, suddenly shifts from my head into my chest. Marie has taught me how yoga views the body as having seven centres or chakras, and I have just fallen into my heart chakra. It's a remarkable feeling: my attention, my centre of awareness, isn't where it usually lives in my brain. The place of 'I am here' is now in my chest. Of course, my brain starts thinking about this, but 'I' can still watch the thoughts happening in my head from this detached perspective. The effect only lasts a minute or two, only for as long as I can sustain the detachment.

Soon the spell is broken and my consciousness shifts back into my head. I feel let down. I wanted to stay in my heart and don't know how to get back. The heart is home to a different sort of consciousness entirely.

I'm reminded that when I left my body in the hospital ward, I'd had a strong physical sensation that my consciousness had made a backflip down my spine, into my heart, before it exploded out through my chest.

*

Another day, something else extraordinary happens. I'm meditating at six o'clock in the morning, the time I usually practise, and I've managed to stop my thoughts.

All of a sudden I rise straight up with no effort at all, as if hinged from my ankles. Arriving in a standing position, I look out of the window. A pigeon perched on the windowsill flies off. I turn around, see myself lying on the floor and, grasping the fact that I'm having another out-of-body experience, I panic.

As soon as I panic I'm sucked back into my body. I open my eyes and locate myself in the room. I'm in a cold sweat, panting with adrenaline from the fright. My etheric body left my physical body and looked out the window. A pigeon flew off as if I'd startled it, which I'm certain must just be a coincidence.

It was like the beginnings of the beyond-death experience, but without any of the trauma. Where would I have gone next if I hadn't panicked? Could I have flown out through the window like I did in the hospital ward? I want to find out, so from then on I practise with greater rigour but with no success.

My etheric body refuses to detach itself again and I'm not surprised. I'm trying to make it happen while my internal dialogue is turned off, but I have to think about it to try, which is a contradiction. And when I'm in the same state of 'not thinking' I can't remember what I did to leave my body the first time. I simply don't know how I did it. All I know is it happened once before in the hospital ward.

*

Marie returns from Nepal and we catch up with what's been happening while she's been away. We drink green tea and I smoke cigarettes while she sits serenely, as motionless as a rock. There's something otherworldly about her presence. She's here, in the room, as physically real and attractive as ever but inside, she's still in the mountains, in a realm I want to access.

I tell her about my yoga practice, how I found myself sinking into my heart, the one time, and levitating out of my body the other. I'm keen to get all the facts right and as usual I'm on a roll. "…and what I don't get is as soon as I have a thought, the whole thing disappears," I click my fingers, "Like that, in a rush, I come back."

"You know what?" asks Marie.

"No, what?"

"You talk too much."

I laugh. She's right. It's samsara. Too much chatter. But I want her to know how much she's helped me. I've found a route back into my beyond-death experience.

"You know when I first told you about my experience, you said you could help me?"

"Yes?"

"Well I just want you to know. You have. More than I can ever tell you."

Marie smiles her enigmatic smile that lets me know I've said enough.

Art College

One evening that same autumn, I'm sitting in a pub with my friend Richard talking about where everyone's going and how they're leaving us behind. It looks to us like a tide of consumerism is sweeping the world and it isn't going to leave any alternatives in its wake. The dreams of retail analysts are coming true: people have indeed 'converted the buying and use of goods into rituals' and 'seek spiritual satisfaction and ego satisfaction in consumption'.

But despite all the goods in the shops, people don't seem to be any happier; in fact the opposite is true. Contentment is in short supply. Consumerism is fuelling inflation, riots and strikes. From where we're sitting, the ideas of the counter culture don't look so bad after all, but they've all been washed away. It doesn't look like there's anything out there for us.

"Can you remember what you really wanted to be when you were a kid?" Richard asks.

"As long as I can remember I wanted to be an artist. Didn't know what you had to do to become one or what it meant to be one, but when other kids wanted to be train drivers or firemen, I wanted to be an artist."

"So why didn't you?"

I told him about my parents refusing their support.

"And?"

"And what?"

"And what's stopping you now?"

"I can't get a grant?"

"Say's who?"

"Says my parents."

"How long have you worked for?"

"Getting on for five years now"

"And you've been paying tax?"

"Yes, it's deducted off my payslips."

"So you qualify for a grant as a mature student. In fact, more than you'd get if you were straight out of school."

I'm dumbfounded. It turns out I've been paying my dues.

Straight away I make a portfolio of my paintings, drawings, doodles and photographs and start applying for foundation courses. I've never thought my attempts to illustrate my beyond-death experience were any good but the interview panels have other ideas.

"So what does this represent?" asks one tutor, staring at a swirl of black tarmac-like paint on a board.

"The dark side," I explain, not wanting to get into it.

"And this?" asks another, turning a white on white canvas around in his hands trying to decide which way up to hold it.

"The Light." I explain. Apparently it's just the sort of thing they want to hear and I get offers from three different colleges.

The space between the atoms

While I wait for Art Colleges to confirm their offers, I'm buried in a library of books. I never imagined this is how my life would pan out – back inside a book. I've come a long way from where I started, on the bus, looking forward to a night out down the Jolly Brewers, without a care in the world aside from my infatuation with Jenny. But here I am. I'm not sure that reading books will lead me back to the places I experienced, but I don't have a choice in the matter.

My intuitive side, the silent mind I've opened up in yoga, accepts my experience and needs no explanations. It's my rational side that won't let it go – the empiricist within me, struggling to fit my journey into the world it understands: a world of land, sea and sky. It needs to make sense of what happened or it'll go crazy trying, and that means finding scientific answers. My reason finds it impossible that the whole of the material world might actually be an illusion. But it can't deny that's where this search is leading.

My head craves explanations; my heart needs none. My intuitive side watches the struggle from the sidelines, slightly bemused, not quite understanding why my reason needs proof when my memories are as clear and incontrovertible as they were the afternoon I returned.

If only my rational mind could map my experience with enough rigour – along with everything else it has encountered, defined, described, labelled and categorised – then the physical and metaphysical might somehow magically mesh together. Everything would fall into place. Maybe my reason is correct and my scientific quest will succeed, but my heart has its doubts.

I've been stuck in my attic studio on Portobello Road night and day as weeks slowly roll into months. My routine is fixed. I rise early. Turn on the heating till I can no longer see my breath condensing in the air. I shower, bundle myself into warm clothes and practice yoga to keep mind and body together. I might restock with fresh provisions from the market downstairs, make a stew that will last for a few days, and then bury myself back in my books.

Friends have stopped calling round. They've given up on me. I know I'm fixated, but if I stop now all the information I've taken in will dissolve into thin air. Nothing's going to stick.

I tell myself I'll just get through the book I'm reading, make my notes and then treat myself to a night out: a frosty walk on Hampstead Heath, a swim in the heated municipal pool. But it doesn't happen. I pick the next book off the shelf from the library I've collected and start on the first page. Marie is back in the mountains. Truck drivers are on strike and jobs from the agency have dried up. It's the beginning of 1979 and the newspapers are calling it the Winter of Discontent.

I'm studying the unintelligible world of quantum physics and it's consumed me for so long I get the feeling that my atoms are scattering. I'm staring at a page of notes and my mind has frozen. The paragraphs no longer hang together. The sentences have lost their meaning. I've been gazing at the words for so long they've started to levitate off the page. They're hanging in space in front of my eyes. I watch them collapse into hundreds of letters. It's bizarre. My concentration was the only thing keeping them together in the first place.

If I take myself, the observer, out of the equation; the letters can do what they like. Left to their own devices it's as if they prefer not to be locked up in words at all. There's more freedom in chaos. They can become themselves and mean what they choose. And before they decide what they're going to spell, their potential is endless. They can become any word in any sentence. Their possibilities are infinite. Just like particles in the world of quantum physics.

Is the quantum universe going to offer me a route into my beyond-death experience? Democritus seemed to think so, he told me to look in the space between the atoms but he's been dead for two and a half thousand years. He was just a voice inside my head.

I'm hung up on my original questions. Quantum mechanics may offer solutions if only I can understand the science. But it sounds so unscientific. It whips the rug out from underneath your feet and leaves you spinning in space. There are no co-ordinates to pin down. Not for the first time there is nothing I recognise as geography.

However, according to modern-day scientists this confounding quantum world governs the universe.

I've got to lay the questions out on a table to be able to see them more clearly. *Where did I go?* is about space, and *Who went there?* is about consciousness.

My consciousness had no physical receptors but still had all its senses intact. The places it went, both good and bad, were as real, even more real than anything in this world of matter, but at the same time less tangible. Not solid.

The world of the demons was smothered in dark. I couldn't see beyond vague shapes. Nonetheless, it contained physical pain and malicious emotions and its own negative logic.

The world of the Light was Home, the source of all life. I experienced it in physical, visible and visceral ways. It was charged with its own positive logic.

In between the Dark and the Light was a grey mist and a black void, no man's land on the way to somewhere else. But places that still need to be located.

And I'd started out in the hospital ward floating above my body, where my consciousness had felt like a tiny piece of ball lightning.

That's what the facts look like laid out on the table.

Which leads me to *How, When* and *Why?*

How is about the physical mechanism that propelled me into other worlds. Was the energy of that ball lightning something to do with it?

When is about the passage of time; the way eternal time worked in the Light and present time works in our space-time continuum. My mind still spins trying to think about that one.

Why is the big question. The one about the purpose of life, but it's unfathomable. What is it to be the eyes and the ears of the Universe?

I should have all the answers but I just have the questions. The more I find out the less I seem to know. 'One thing only I know and that is, I know nothing.' I can thank Socrates for that maxim. But it wasn't like that in the Light. Every answer was laid out in rippling waves of understanding. And at the centre of the pond where the questioning stones landed: 'Wisdom is Love. Love is Wisdom'. It was the Light's most profound message but its meaning drifts further and further away the more time distances me.

Trying to find answers in the books of our material world is probably the wrong place to look. I need someone with a bat to whack me on the head every time I try and compare the laws of this world with the laws of that. But my reason isn't listening and that's why I'm here in my studio, surrounded by a small library, looking for the space between the atoms.

*

Just thinking about the size of an atom is mind-blowing. If Democritus were around today he'd be astonished how small his 'a-toma' really are. I try to get a handle on it. I imagine a ladder of scale. At the top are really large things like planets. I only have to descend a few rungs to arrive at everyday things like mountains and another three rungs to encounter humans. Three rungs further down is a grain of sand but I have to climb down seven more rungs before I reach an atom. Half a million of them, lined up shoulder to shoulder, could hide behind a human hair. And they aren't 'un-cuttable' as Democritus thought. Nothing is un-cuttable.

The further I descend down the ladder, the more things that can be called solid disappear. The outer shell of an atom is made of a cloud of electrons, but where they actually are at any one time is impossible to say. They're potentially everywhere at once. Inside the atom sits the nucleus, so small that if an atom were the size of a cathedral, its nucleus would be a fly hovering in the middle of the nave. But the fly would be heavier than the whole cathedral.

Five rungs further down the ladder are protons and neutrons, the building blocks of the nucleus. They both repel and attract each other, caught in a never-ending battle to break free. They fight their containment so vigorously that they spin around and around at 40,000 miles a second. The speeds are incomprehensible inside something so small.

And to finally quash Democritus's idea of a solid, un-cuttable atom, ninety-nine point nine per cent of the space inside an atom is completely empty. So what happens to matter if most of the stuff that matter is made of is empty space?

Parmenides reasoned that nothing could be empty, since in his unchanging and unchangeable world, any void would already be filled. Apparently he was wrong, but what if he was correct, too? Far down in the recesses of that emptiness, something is bubbling and boiling over.

Climbing another five rungs down the ladder, sub-atomic elements like quarks and leptons behave either as particles or as waves depending, bizarrely, on how they feel at the time and who is looking at them. It's illogical, but waves can be particles and particles can be waves.

The Standard Model of Particle Physics, the best description of the quantum world that physicists have arrived at so far, sounds completely counter-intuitive. Not only can sub-atomic particles change from behaving like particles to behaving like waves, they can pop into space from out of nowhere and disappear again just as easily. To go anywhere they first travel everywhere. They can exist in all places at any time but can't be pinned down to any one of them. They can affect each other instantaneously across vast spaces, ignoring the fact that nothing is supposed to be able to travel faster than the speed of light. And to cap it all, there are no certainties of where they are in the quantum world, only probabilities.

So the Standard Model is not that simple. It includes the elusive Higg's Boson and a universe of anti-matter that haven't yet been found, and it doesn't include gravity that has yet to find its place. Apart from that, it's the best description physicists have so far.

*

This is why my mind has frozen. Thoughts ping into existence a bit like particles and hang there waiting to be connected into sentences that might follow some sort of logic in this illogical quantum realm.

A particle cloud of words circles my head – thousands and thousands of letters. I remember a quote from the famous quantum physicist, Niels Bohr, 'If a person is not outraged on first hearing quantum theory, they don't understand what has been said.'

I'm outraged. But I'm also on to something. It feels tantalisingly close, like it's always been there, just out of my reach. What if the metaphysical world that I perceived as the size of a universe was in fact everywhere but took up no space at all? What if the void I've been searching for, the place I disappeared into, isn't in outer space like Pythagoras's spheres. What if it's here? Right here in this room in the space between the atoms. I should be able to reach out and touch it. Just like that.

In my mind's eye, the room is blasted apart as if caught in the centre of a particle accelerator. Walls, floor and ceiling disintegrate into a cloud of billions of particles swarming like tornadoes, circling like galaxies, at speeds too fast to follow. As I watch, the particles clump together. Some are attracted to each other. Some are repelled. Some form gaseous clouds, orbiting around themselves. The particles swarm like clouds of starlings.

If I could have seen myself when I became nothing more than a piece of ball lightning, is this what my consciousness would have looked like, swarming above my lifeless body?

*

There are two things about quantum mechanics that offer an opening for my quest. The first is interference. Sub-atomic particles behave like wave fronts and when they encounter other wave fronts they create interference patterns like two ripples colliding on the surface of a lake.

The second is entanglement. When two particles from the same source become entangled they will still reflect each other and behave as one and the same, even if separated by galactic distances.

I remember the screens in my life review containing the memories of my existence. They were like 3D holographic images, each memory played out in its allotted timeframe. What if each memory was an input of information into my brain in the form of a wave front, and when it collided with the wave fronts already there – existing memory waves – they formed an interference pattern. A holographic image locked in the brain in exactly that point of the space-time continuum. Each interference pattern would be frozen in the region of space-time where the experience took place.

And entanglement means that my connection with each memory would never be lost and that's how the Light Beings were able to call them up and pick and choose which they wanted me to see.

If this idea isn't mind-bending enough it provides the key to a second idea: quantum entanglement could mean that all the billions of sub-atomic particles inside my brain are linked and can't be separated. If my mind is a bunch of entangled particles, they will still be entangled when their host, my brain, is switched off. And my mind will still be connected to all the interference patterns that make up the holographic universe of memories – millions upon millions of sensory inputs. So even though my consciousness left my body it might still be attached in some way to its life experiences.

The way I see it, the entangled sub-atomic particles are not separated by galactic distances. They aren't even separated by the distance between Kingston and Kew where most of my life has played out. Space is just the construct in the space-time continuum that gives us the illusion that places are separate. They are not. Behind this illusion is the entangled quantum universe. So where is it?

I'm watching the particle cloud swirling in the space my room used to inhabit. The room is still here and I'm still sitting in it but the illusion of space has shattered. I have projected myself into a universe of atoms. Inside the universe I am a tiny solar system, a cluster of sub-atomic particles.

I'm beginning see a solution for my map. I've been looking for a destination outside of myself but the metaphysical world is everywhere. It's all around us all the time. It's like trying to find America on a map of America. I can't find the continent because I can't see where it begins or ends. The whole map is America. I didn't need to travel galactically. I could have travelled sub-atomically. When I left my body I may have continued to exist as a condensation of waves. Waves attracted to themselves by the glue that stuck me together.

The continent I've been looking for is almost on the last rung of my ladder: thirty-five rungs below the scale of a human, twenty-five below an atom, fifteen below elementary particles.

Underlying everything – mountains and whales, molecules and atoms, protons and neutrons, quarks and leptons – there is something constant. A bubbling, boiling sea of energy called the unified or zero point field.

Max Planck, one of the gods of quantum physics, discovered the field in 1900. On discovering it, he came to this conclusion:

All matter originates and exists only by virtue of a force which brings the particle of an atom to vibration and holds this most minute solar system of the atom together. We must assume behind this force the existence of a conscious and intelligent mind. This mind is the matrix of all matter.

He called it 'zero point' as it's the energy remaining at absolute zero in a vacuum, or as close to that as is possible. And he called it 'unified' because it is patterned like a fabric – a matrix that is everywhere. Even in a vacuum at zero degrees, as close to an empty space as it's possible to get.

The physicist John Archibald Wheeler described the zero point field as 'a foamy sea of constantly emerging particles and anti-particles of immense intrinsic energy which come into existence spontaneously and then annihilate themselves.' These particles move at speeds of ten to the power of minus forty-three seconds. So something very small indeed is appearing and disappearing very, very fast. And it's doing it literally everywhere all the time.

Not only is it everywhere all the time, but it contains far more intrinsic energy than any nuclear explosion. There's enough energy in one cubic metre of the field to boil all the oceans of the world. There shouldn't be anything there, but there is. Is this where the metaphysical universe is located, in the space between the atoms?

The waves in this foaming sea exist in a world of multiple possibilities. When a wave collapses, sub-atomic particles are released. These particles manifest out of the quantum world of infinite possibilities into our physical world of finite probabilities. In other words, the waves collapse into matter. That's where the stuff that makes us and everything else comes from.

This is the science.

But is this where I went?

If the origins of matter are to be found in the zero point field, then consciousness could be created at a quantum level too. A cloud of sub-atomic particles that condenses in the brain, straight from the foamy quantum sea.

Then when the brain stops providing the life support system it needs, consciousness leaves in an entangled cloud – a concentration of consciousness, and flies back into the sea from where it came.

The Light and everything it contained might be located in the fabric of the unified field. The clouds and the Light Beings, the lakes of infinite wisdom containing all the knowledge of the universe, the Source, the river of life, and the cities of light; everything.

Which means the current I was swimming in, drawing me through the black void into the Light, was the force of the foamy quantum sea welcoming me back. As if I were a droplet of water attracted by the companionship of a whole ocean.

The Indian man

In 1965, the sight of an Indian man in Kingston-upon-Thames was unusual, exotic even. The Indian man I passed most days at the age of eight, walking by myself to and from school, represented for me all the exciting characters from a world entirely out of my reach – Kim and Mowgli, Aladdin, Ali Baba, Sinbad, endless possibilities of escape from my boring, flatland suburban sameness.

At the time, this Indian man seemed ancient beyond years, though in reality he was probably in his sixties. He dressed in a creased linen suit with shirt and tie, no socks or shoes, even in winter. He had a shambling gait, long hair and a beard, and his glasses were stuck together with Elastoplast. More extraordinary than his appearance was the way he touched everything in his path and mumbled to it. Bushes, trees, gateposts, fences, street-lamps, the post box, each received a light touch, a series of nods and a mumbled incantation. Flowers got his special attention.

I asked my Dad what he was up to and he said it was his religion and that fascinated me even more. "What do you mean his religion?" I asked.

"Well, not everybody believes in science, especially if they come from foreign parts."

"So what religion is he?"

"I don't know, you'll have to ask him," Dad was winding me up, knowing full well I'd been taught not to talk to strangers and didn't have the tools to introduce myself, let alone ask him something so personal.

"He's probably some sort of Hindu," Dad went on, "They believe everything in the world is sacred. Some Hindus are vegetarian; they won't kill anything, not even an ant in their path. They have to brush the street ahead clean of bugs before they can walk on it. Your Indian is probably one of those. He's blessing the plants."

"But he blesses the lampposts too."

"Well, they light up the streets don't they?"

"But he blesses the post box."

"Well why not? It sends your mail where you want it to go, doesn't it?"

I couldn't argue with that and left it there.

Whenever our paths crossed as I walked to and from school I used to stalk the Indian man, always a good way behind, out of sight. I was gripped by a peculiar thrill at the thought of being caught. What would he do? Would he touch me too? Would I be blessed? Too full of questions for my own good, as my father used to say.

*

Many years later I'm reading up on Indian religions and come across Jainism, a religion much older than Hinduism. I feel sure that this must be the Indian man's faith. The way my father thought they 'blessed' things they passed wasn't exactly what was happening. They weren't so much blessing things as bringing them into being, affirming their existence.

Jainists believe that we bring the world into existence by our own acts of consciousness. We play an active and most crucial part in the very creation of the world – this is the duty their followers must fulfil by affirming the existence of everything they encounter.

I wish aged eight that I'd been able to talk to that Indian man.

I wish I'd had the presence of mind or words in my head to ask him what he was doing because, fourteen years later, it turns out that the Indian from 1965 wasn't nearly as crazy as he looked. In fact, in the most fundamental way, in calling the world into existence on a daily basis he was conscientiously doing what all of us do unknowingly every second of every day, all of the time.

If only we knew it.

Consciousness

In the Records Office of Queen Mary's Hospital, Roehampton, the secretary asks me if she can help. I hand her a letter of introduction from my GP and explain how I'm interested in looking at my notes from when I was in theatre during my cardiac arrest. I'm sure my quest is too far out there for her so when she asks why I'm interested I say I'm trying to fill in the gaps, flesh out the details.

"There won't be many details," she says, "No one's taking notes in theatre when someone has a cardiac arrest. But I'll look anyway."

She disappears into the filing rooms and I wait, wondering why I've retraced my steps back here to the hospital. I'm hoping they'll be something in my file to clarify my questions about consciousness. I don't expect the answer to be sitting there in my notes, but maybe I'll find some little detail I've overlooked that will open up a new avenue. Point me in a different direction.

I'm still looking for scientific answers and I figure a hospital is a good place to find them. I've come to realise that this exploration hasn't really been about satisfying any doubts, seeing as I can't dispute that my beyond-death experience happened. It's actually been about trying to fit the limits of the material world into the greater scheme of things that I encountered in the Light.

And, more truthfully, my search hasn't even been about satisfying my thirst for logic as I've thought it was all along; it's been about appeasing the voice inside my head that is my father. His detached, objective way of looking at the world in the cold light of day. The way he has taught me to think instead of feel.

But thinking is only one way of knowing, and without the capacity to feel the sensations that bring facts to life, it is a parched existence. I remember the Light Being's advice, "Only through the mind can the world be seen. Only through the heart can it be understood."

My quest has brought me back to where I started. My books about quantum mechanics have led me to believe that events lost in time can be locked in space. That to revisit a place, to repeat a journey, can unlock these events, shed light on them and, I hope, finally locate the joins, the crossings and the borders of my map.

The secretary returns with my notes. She's correct. There's a breakdown of the drugs I was given, a record of the time resuscitation took – nine minutes – and nothing else, not even the number of times they had to shock my heart. I'm disappointed. There are no leads here.

I stand there staring at her blankly, not grasping that it's time for me to leave when she asks, "Did something else happen to you that you don't understand?"

It's such an unexpected and curious question from a secretary in a records department that for a moment it doesn't register, and when it does I say,

"Yes. You could say that. Something I've spent the last five years trying to understand."

She waits for me to go on, so I describe, as briefly as I can, my out of body experience in the ward up until the point when everything disappeared and I entered the grey mist.

Instead of the disbelief I expect, she says, "Please take a seat and wait a minute. There's someone who would like to talk to you." She picks up a phone, scans a list of numbers and makes a call. "He'll just be a few minutes, if that's all right?"

A man in a white coat arrives. He looks to be in his early forties, Arabic, a fine angular nose, olive skin, neat beard. But he hasn't come to take me away.

"Hello, are you Mr Booth?" he asks.

"Yes?" I answer suspiciously.

"My name is Dr Karim Akhtar, I wonder if we can have a chat."

"OK."

"I work here as a cardiologist, but in my own country my training is in neuroscience. I am interested in interviewing patients who have questions arising from the experience of a cardiac arrest. That's why the secretary paged me."

He sits down next to me in the Records Office and we have the most extraordinary conversation. He pulls out a notepad, takes down my details and asks about my experience. He listens as I talk, prompting me for more information at every step as if he's making a diagnosis of an everyday occurrence, interrupting to ask questions and request clarifications, while making copious notes.

When I've finished he asks, "And what brought you here today?" I describe how I'm searching for an explanation – how my consciousness could leave my body – that's led to trying to define consciousness: what it is; how, for me, it's the elephant in the room that science doesn't like to talk about.

Dr Karim Akhtar doesn't belittle my crazy ideas. Instead, he suggests we reconvene in the staff canteen for some lunch. I'm in a slight state of shock that this is happening, but I follow him down a maze of corridors till we arrive at the canteen. We take our lunch out into the garden. The same garden where my journey started five years ago.

We sit on a bench and he explains, "As I said, my training is in neuroscience, so if you have any questions I can help you with, please ask."

Without a thought as to why he should be giving me his time, I plough straight into my questions: What is consciousness? How can my mind travel outside of its shut-down brain? Where did I go?

A wry smile crosses his face, "It seems you have been asking the same questions I, and at some time or another, every neuroscientist in the world, has asked themselves about where consciousness is located, and the answer is we are as much in the dark as you are."

I look at him dumbfounded. I don't expect this sort of candour from a doctor.

"All we know about consciousness is that it has something to do with the head, rather than the foot."

That gets a laugh from me.

"There are of course paradigms we work to – that consciousness is the product of neuronal networks, that we can follow the circuitry down through the dendrites and synapses to the neurons or brain cells and inside the brain cells, through the DNA, RNA, to the genes. And current paradigms dictate that genetic forces inside each and every brain cell somehow motivate consciousness. That's the science and there's no room for thinking outside of the box. That is if you want to work in the mainstream."

He stops to take a bite from his sandwich and chews deliberately while he thinks.

"So consciousness must be a product, even a by-product, of electromagnetic interference. But I for one, and plenty of other neuroscientists don't actually believe the paradigms. Cells can't talk to each other – they don't have a language other than chemical exchange – and the genes locked inside each cell have even less opportunity to communicate. In relation to each cell, the brain is the size of a universe. For genes to be able to talk to the brain would be like us being able to talk to the next galaxy."

"We work with the paradigms, as they're the only cards we're holding in our hands. Unfortunately, the more neuroscience discovers, the less we understand."

That sounds familiar. It sounds like Socrates' maxim.

"Scanners are so sensitive these days that they can map the tiniest part of the brain…" He swigs his coffee and takes another bite from his sandwich.

"But…?"

"But they haven't found the seat of consciousness. Scanners can tell where things are going on but not what's going on there. We can see the flow of consciousness – when and where it happens – but not the content. We can ask our subjects what they're thinking and can identify where they're thinking it, but only with the most simple of exercises. Identifying 'yes' and 'no' decision centres is a long way from unravelling consciousness. The complexity of brain activity engaged in something we find as simple as language, for instance, is phenomenal.

"The problem with looking for consciousness by reducing the brain to the sum of its parts is that the brain doesn't function as individual parts. It functions en masse as a self-regulating unit. Consciousness is something that only becomes apparent when all the different parts, from gene to neuron, from dendrites to cerebellum, are firing on all cylinders. If the theories don't allow for something as large as the brain to be able to contain a mind then how are things as tiny as genes supposed to contain the mind? Even if the mind is nothing more than an illusion of 'self' produced by the brain – and I for one don't belong in that camp."

Seeing the rapt expression on my face, he continues, "If the choices of the 'mind' are simply an illusion of 'free will' imparted somehow to the brain by its neuronal networks, how do those neuronal networks organise themselves without a sense of self? Without the controlling influence of a mind?"

I think I'm getting it, so I interject. "You can't ask a gene to organise a dinner party let alone write a PhD."

Dr Karim Akhtar laughs, "Precisely. Then there's the problem of the longevity of the self. Every neuron is eighty per cent water with around a hundred thousand molecules swimming around in it. It takes a hundred billion such neurons to make a brain, making ten to the power of fifteen molecules. Each neuron is linked to its neighbours by at least ten thousand connections. Now the molecules in every neuron are replaced around ten thousand times in a lifetime. And yet we have a continuous sense of self that is stable over time."

"But all the scaffolding supporting the self has been taken down and replaced many times over?" I ask.

"Exactly. The scaffolding has been demolished and rebuilt but the builder is still standing, apparently in thin air."

"I know nothing about neuroscience." I admit, "I'm not even a qualified scientist. If anything, I'm coming from a philosophical perspective…"

"Yes? And what does philosophy tell us?"

"It gives us three choices, more or less. Materialists believe that everything, including consciousness, is the product of matter. Dualists believe that consciousness is an entity separate from the brain – mind and matter – and idealists believe that the only thing that exists is consciousness – and that the physical world is an illusion of our senses."

"And which do you believe?"

"I'm not sure it's a question of belief. For me it's a question of looking for the theory that most closely matches the evidence. I returned from my beyond-death experience as an idealist though it took me a long time to find out what that meant, philosophically that is. And while I was looking the world slowly solidified around me and I became more of a dualist. Recently through meditation I've begun to drift back into the idealist camp. Everything is an illusion of perception inside our space-time continuum."

He pauses.

"Very interesting, but I'm a scientist not a philosopher."

"So what are the options in science?"

Dr Karim Akhtar gives me a considered look while he drinks his coffee and chews his sandwich, "Consciousness is either a product of cerebral activity – neuronal networks – or it's associated with neuronal quantum processes."

"Neuronal quantum processes?"

"Yes, that quantum processes are occurring inside our brains that link us to a quantum field."

I feel the spark of infinity. The hairs stand up on the back of my neck.

"That link us to a matrix?" I ask.

"Well that's what Max Planck called it." Dr Karim Akhtar has clearly been reading the same books as me. "Yes, a matrix. So consciousness could be a neuronal quantum process that reverts back into the quantum field.

"Or...and this is your idealist proposition: Mind is as fundamental a component of the universe as elementary particles and forces."

"An elemental force?"

"Yes. Consciousness could be a force like gravity or electromagnetism that can't be broken down into components of other forces. It's elemental."

It feels like stars are exploding inside my head. "So, outside of the quantum field?"

"Inside? Outside? Who knows? At this level of thought, terms like these lose their meaning. 'Elemental' means that consciousness could be a separate entity, irreducible in terms of brain function. An energy force the brain can channel. The brain doesn't necessarily generate consciousness. All the information it processes is external. All our senses are external. The brain itself has no nerve endings. It could simply be a filter for the mind that, while we are alive, links us to the space-time continuum."

"Like a TV set?" I blurt it out. The analogy has just popped into my head but I haven't thought it through.

He raises his eyebrows, "A TV set? I don't understand."

"Well, we tune a TV set to separate channels that filter out all the white noise getting in the way of the signal. Could the brain operate like that?"

He gets it, "Yes, not only tuning our brains to one channel of reality but also limiting our consciousness from being overwhelmed by a cacophony of different signals."

"From the white noise of reality."

He smiles at the analogy. "Yes, from being overwhelmed by the white noise of reality. For a long time I've thought we might need a brand new branch of science – a science of consciousness. Physicists at the cutting edge of 'pure' science no longer believe that materialism can explain the universe. Quantum physics put an end to such easy notions."

Dr Karim Akhtar stops talking and we both eat our lunch as I take in the science. I begin to feel the weight of five years lifting off my shoulders. A scientific answer, even if it's only a hypothesis, seems within my grasp. His wry smile returns to his face as he watches the impression he has made on mine.

"Mind blowing stuff. Yes?" he says.

I laugh out loud in delight. People in the garden turn and stare at us. "Yes, mind blowing stuff. You've just shed light on the mystery I've been trying to solve for five years."

"Only for five years? There are many who have worked on this mystery for a lot longer than that."

I realise I sound precocious.

"It's an obsession. Since my experience I've been trying to find scientific answers to explain what happened to me."

"Scientific proof. Yes, it's a hard taskmaster."

We've both finished our lunch and Dr Karim Akhtar offers me one of his Turkish cigarettes. We light up and smoke.

He smiles contentedly, "You've been asking all the right questions, but there's one you haven't asked me yet."

I rack my brains thinking what it could be.

"I'm sorry I can't think. What is it?"

"It is this. Why am I here talking to you? Why are we here, sitting in this garden over lunch on a sunny day talking with each other about the metaphysics of life?"

Of course, that's the question I should be asking.

"So?" I ask.

"So what?" he asks. He wants me to spell it out for him. So I do: "Why are you here listening to my account of a bizarre, far-fetched, incredible journey when as a medical professional I expect you to be calling the psych ward."

"That is a good question..." he stares at me, "It is because of this..." he pauses while he smokes, keeping me hooked, "It is because I too have taken the same journey as you."

My jaw drops. All this time spent by myself, working alone in a wilderness of unconventional ideas, swimming against the tide of opinion, sometimes drowning in isolation.

"Please. Tell me." I ask.

"I am conducting research, not in my capacity as a cardiologist you understand, outside of my professional commitments. I have asked some of the staff in the hospital that when they hear of people like yourself – and there are others; not many – that they get in touch so I can interview them, like I have interviewed you. It is my own personal research and comes from an interest; no, not an interest, an obsession, like your own. But the staff I have asked are not my peers, they are not consultants or registrars. If consultants knew what I was doing it might prejudice my position."

I wait while he smokes and stares pensively at the sky.

"I was a trainee doctor in Persia, my country – now, no longer... now, the Iran of the mullahs – when, like you, I suffered a cardiac arrest. I was brain-dead, but like you I did not die. I followed the black tunnel into the Light, the same as you. I was in the Light and nothing could have made me leave, but I was pulled back through the black void. The tunnel was like an umbilical cord and I realised that each of us is connected to the different dimension in the Light by this umbilical cord. Even while we are alive, we are still connected somehow, I don't know how. The Light is a dimension where the whole universe is a giant energy field. And in an eternal time zone of always now."

"Do you mean the zero point field? Or a matrix?" I ask.

"Yes, maybe Planck's matrix."

"Please. Tell me." I say again, "What happened in the Light?" I am beside myself wanting to know. But just like me a few years before, Dr Karim Akhtar is unwilling to open up.

"Many things and I have not the time to tell you half of them. The doctors thought I was dead and put me in the mortuary, lying on a trolley, covered in a sheet. I came round an hour and a half later."

I want to hug him but it's not appropriate. He stands up, shakes my hand, thanks me for my time and says he has to get back to work. The garden is emptying as staff finish their lunch. It has taken me so long to find someone like myself I don't want him to leave. I stall for time.

"Just one more thing before you go."

"Yes?"

"You've had the same experience as me. You've seen the other side. What do you do with that?"

"What do I do with that?" he seems not to understand.

"How do you square that other universe with this one? Knowing what you know."

He stops to think, then looks straight at me. It feels like he's looking right inside me.

"I live," he says. He waits to see if his lesson is sinking in. Two words that will release me from my search. "Life is finite until you die and then you enter infinity. Don't let one get in the way of the other."

It's what I've been doing these past five years, letting my beyond-death experience get in the way of living. A life lived without a thought of death is an undervalued life, but a life spent thinking about little else is no life at all. Dr Karim Akhtar looks at me as if he can read these thoughts connecting in my mind. A smile breaks across my face at his revelation, and another smile breaks across his at my understanding.

"Please, can I contact you?" I ask.

He passes me his notepad, "Write your address. I'll see what I can do."

While I'm scribbling my address down on his notepad he asks me a favour, "You say 'please' and I will ask the same. Please do not talk about what has happened here today. I am a medical professional and a foreigner. I cannot let my position become compromised by crazy, metaphysical ideas... even if we both know the true nature of things."

"But it's taken me so long to find someone who has had the same experience..." I plead.

He looks at me with deep understanding, "Yes, I know what that feels like. And now you have. Met someone, that is. And I have too. Met another person like myself. I have your details. I will be in touch." He bows, almost imperceptibly but it's there, and then he's gone. I sit by myself in the empty garden where my journey started, tears of happiness rolling down my face.

Back on the bus

Leaving Queen Mary's Hospital, I catch the bus to Richmond Park. It's five years since I last found myself sitting in my favourite seat at the back of the top-deck. At that time I was adrift, rudderless, and looked to the Park for a reassuring mooring on which to fix my existence: physically solid and undeniably real. Now, the tables have turned.

While in my core, I feel as invincible as ever, the solidity of the Park along with everything else in our three dimensional space-time continuum is less certain. From a quantum perspective, trees and grass, wood and heath are no longer as dependable as they first appeared.

No matter. I want to walk in the fresh air. My meeting with Dr Karim Akhtar has blown me away. I've always suspected there must be other people who have taken the same journey and remembered being there. But to actually meet someone in this world, face-to-face. That's something.

From the start, the thing that has marked my own journey has been isolation. First, collapsing in the street, at home through the weekend waiting for someone to take my condition seriously, and in the hospital ward trying to hit the panic button. Then, finding myself alone in the grey mist and single-handedly fighting the forces of evil. The guardian aided my escape, but he wasn't a companion. I was in awe of his magnificence and authority, yet anxious he'd drop me back into the Dark.

It wasn't till I encountered the Light and found companionship with the Light Beings, one of whom was a long-forgotten friend, that my sense of isolation was broken. But when I returned to the physical world so did the isolation. I found myself alone in a strange world I no longer understood and, searching for a scientific explanation for my experience, all along I'd been in a research group of one.

The Light Beings warned me against talking about their world and they were right; that way lies incomprehension and ridicule. But they also left a clue in my consciousness – "Only a few can remember where they come from" – and by chance or design, I don't know or care which, I had been lucky enough to meet some of the few who helped me break my solitude.

Linda, who remembered choosing her mother before she was born; Marie, whose own spiritual search leads her towards the same destinations as my own; and Dr Karim Akhtar, a witness to the same extraordinary metaphysical universe as myself.

And there are others. When I stop to think about it I also need to count the many books of philosophers and scientists: the imaginary friends I've made along the way who have asked the same difficult questions. It makes me laugh that I used to think the world can't be found in a book and now I can't do without them.

I reach an open heath in the park and collapse in tussocks of grass. It's been a long journey and I'm exhausted. I knew from the beginning this was always going to be a personal search. There weren't any passengers I could invite along. But now I've met passengers – other people who understand where I'm coming from. A wave of happiness washes over me. I'm not alone. Lying in the grass staring at the sky, I feel like I've finally come back.

The brighter the light...

From the top of a ridge in Richmond Park the suburban sprawl of Kingston-upon-Thames pans out below me. It's the landscape of my childhood. Through a coin-slot telescope I can pick out the places where the events of my life have taken place. But the places are just spaces; they know nothing of the events that happened there. Those events are in an entirely different place, locked in time.

The coin in the telescope runs out of time, the eyepiece clunks shut and I sit down on a park bench. The afternoon sun is bright but there's still a winter nip to the air. Daffodils carpet the hillside in yellow. A couple have brought scraps to feed birds, and flocks of pigeons and sparrows descend on them. A mum pushes an empty buggy along a tarmac path while her toddler makes his own path of footprints in newly turned flowerbeds. She sits down on the bench to watch her toddler play. An old war veteran, smartly dressed in blazer and tie, dozes in his wheelchair, medals on his chest, a blanket over his lap. It feels like a long time since I've paid attention to these little details of everyday life. I've missed them.

But before I take Dr Karim Akhtar's advice and get on with living, I still have one burning question; the one that has driven me more than any other. It's the fear of being caught in the world of the demonic humans next time round that has really haunted me for the last five years.

Why had I found myself in the grip of purest evil?

Where can I place the Dark on my map and in my understanding of what lies beyond death?

I've reached an answer of sorts. Not one that I like and not one I can verify, but at least one that keeps the demons from my door right now.

In Plato's account, Er described the Dark as two cave mouths descending into the earth. Those who were allowed to escape came out haggard and wretched, reporting terrible experiences, while those who weren't allowed out were condemned in perpetuity.

On the banks of the Nile, Plotinus imagined the flickering light of souls detaching themselves from dark bodies and returning to the light of the One. The ones who didn't had drifted too far away from its source during their lives. They were forever lost in the Dark.

From his mountain retreat in the heart of nature, living the life of a hermit, Heraclitus divined that it's only the constant flux and flow from one opposite to another that makes life possible. Nature is made of opposites.

And standing on the city heights of Athens, surveying the world through the clarity of his logic, Parmenides reasoned that the Dark was an elemental force. The universe existed in a fixed state where two forces – the aether and ignorant night – were immeasurably intertwined. I marvel at his description. A logical deduction from so long ago that gets to me still. The aether and ignorant night, good and bad, so closely woven together, intertwined like a double helix.

So far, so good for the physical world of matter: a world dependent on dualities like space and time. But what about the metaphysical world? Outside of space and time where time was ever-present, eternal, and space was everywhere, anywhere. Does the metaphysical have to obey the same law of opposites?

The answer had been there all these years and I didn't see it because I hadn't wanted to look. Could it be that the Light and the Dark are balancing each other? It's a chilling thought. The aether and ignorant night, immeasurably intertwined, as dependent on each other as space is on time. Good and evil, love and hate, wisdom and ignorance, terror and security, excruciating pain and unimaginable ecstasy, each the opposite of the other and each in balance with the other?

The Light was brighter than ten thousand suns, which gives me a horrifying sense of the how evil the Dark could have become if I'd fallen any further into its depths. The brighter the light, the darker its shadow.

Maybe that's why the Light Beings found it distasteful to talk about the Dark. Perhaps that's why they didn't want to dwell on it or for me to remember. It was too close to home.

Up until now, I've thought of the realm of the demonic humans as a minor, inferior place compared to the superior realm of the Light: a transit-stop on my journey. But now I redraw the two realms as equal and opposite, one balancing the other.

I wanted my map to be based solely on my own experience. That's all I had to go on. But despite my lone efforts I arrive at the same place Christian, Buddhist, Hindu and other religions reached a long time ago. My map is beginning to look like other religious maps of the afterlife and there's something in that; it's an affirmation. I'm not about to join one of the old religions, preaching outdated dogmas for their own sustenance. I'm not about to claim my way is any way at all, seeing as all I know in this world is Socrates' edict; "One thing only I know and that is, I know nothing." Nonetheless, it's reassuring to discover we share common ground.

If the Light and the Dark are really immeasurably intertwined, I've found a place for the Dark. It is at the very least as good an explanation as I need for my own peace of mind. But it's one thing to find a location and another altogether to explain the forces that ensnared me.

*

The Light manifested as universal love and compassion, wisdom and joy. The Dark was fed by the opposite: hatred, cruelty, ignorance, malice and spite. I figure all these negative energies must have one thing in common, one thing that unites them. It's taken me a long time to come up with an answer and now that I have, I could kick myself. It's so obvious: fear. Fear is the absence of love. It repels positive energy and dispels hope. The fear I encountered in the Dark almost drained the life out of me.

According to psychologists there are five fears we all experience: fear of annihilation, fear of mutilation, fear of abandonment, fear of entrapment, and fear of the disintegration of the self: the death of our ego. When I died I experienced all five.

First annihilation and mutilation came together, with the cardiac arrest and loss of my body, floating above the husk I'd left behind. But once I realised I hadn't been annihilated I wasn't scared. I was fascinated. I was the kernel threshed out of the husk.

Second, I experienced abandonment in the grey mist, that's when fear had really started to take hold.

Then came entrapment, as I was smothered by the demonic humans, unable to escape.

Which lead to the loss of the integrity of my self as their minds invaded my own like a virus.

But I didn't turn into one of the demonic humans. I discovered some inner strength I'd never known I had, as well as some intuition as to what I had to do to escape. Even though I had no idea that focussing on the possibility of love for all that was good and true and right in existence would attract the help of the guardian who rescued me.

It sounds bizarre that the demonic humans who trapped me in their world of unfathomable evil could also be afraid. But it was true. As my thoughts became enmeshed in theirs I'd found them experiencing fear too. They were trapped themselves, by far crueller masters who were directing their minions from the depths. Any capacity for love had been completely drained out of them and with it, any chance of escape. The demons had chosen to be that way, to join the cohorts of malice. A choice I can only presume they practised in life and now reflected in death. Behind their bravado, they knew it too.

It's hard to square their hatred and cruelty with the idea that they were living in fear, but the more I think about it the plainer it becomes. Fear was at the root of whatever vindictiveness they brought to bear on me.

First I look at hate. The demonic humans hated me. Why? Because they couldn't stand any beings that were not like themselves. Why not? Because I possessed something that they had lost: love. They wanted to prevent me from discovering that love is stronger than hate. That light dispels the dark.

Next I look at cruelty. Why did they take pleasure in being cruel? Because that's what they'd learnt in life. But why had they learnt it? Because of the sense of power it gave them. And why did they need power over others? Because they were afraid. What were they frightened of? Themselves, their place in the world and the place they'd end up.

And why did they fear me? Because I had something they wanted besides love: freedom. I hadn't joined their cohorts or lost the integrity of my self. I still had a choice. For them, it was already too late.

The more I follow these thoughts, the more things fall into place. I look at Er's account again and find the same link to fear: desperate and haggard people, fearful of what lay below, begged to be allowed out through the cave mouths. But there were some – the psychopaths, mass murderers and tyrants – who were too evil ever to be released. However hard they tried to escape, the fiery guards would chase them back into the depths of the underworld. Both those who escaped and those who didn't shared one thing in common. Fear.

As for why I'd found myself in the Dark, whether it was an unresolved past or a terrifying present, I still can't be sure. But what I am sure about is that, one way or another, I'd been trapped by my own fears.

When the writhing mass of demons caught up with me I'd already been waiting in the grey mist for far too long. A horror had begun to grow inside me – horror that this limbo was where you went for ever and there was nothing else. I was totally isolated, not knowing what to do or what would come next. I was hanging on to my attachment to life. I wasn't ready to die; it was all a big mistake, I was too young. All these thoughts were obstacles to letting go and the strongest was the unrequited love I felt for Jenny. I know now that it was a romantic illusion, one that kept me longing for the world of flesh and blood instead of accepting the world of the dead, but at the time it was enough to keep me there.

The mechanics of my escape are becoming clearer. As Heraclitus says, flux and flow are essential to the dynamism of any system, so there must be an exchange between the Dark and the Light. In Er's account there were those who were allowed to climb out of the caves and ascend into the Elysian Fields. I too was part of that exchange. The key was to stay positive and hopeful, the feelings the demons most wanted to erode. I had the presence of mind to make a conscious choice, and I've a gut feeling this was crucial to my escape. The Light didn't come of its own accord. It had to be chosen.

Caught in the darkness, I appealed for help from all the positive energy in Creation. I was rescued by the guardian and lifted towards the Light. Had I succumbed to fear, it's likely my journey would have taken a very different route. But I had an intuitive knowledge that there is love in Nature and I focused on that core belief.

As my thoughts became enmeshed with those of the demonic humans, what I learnt about their world holds true for the world of the living. People are conduits for energy through their thoughts, their words and their deeds. Negative thoughts, words and deeds create negative energy that doesn't go away. It feeds the Dark. I don't know how it works. I just know that's how it is.

Some people enjoy hurting others as it makes them feel more powerful. Some people bully others to make up for their own insecurities. Some people set out to get the better of everyone else. Smarmy salesmen demanding we make consumption our way of life, all the while lining their own pockets, tricking naïve and fair-minded people until they've lost the little they had. And when these salesmen of consumerism have climbed over everyone in their path to get to the top, even that's not enough for them. They also want the moral high ground and say things like, 'It's progress', 'The end justifies the means', 'It's survival of the fittest' or 'That's the way of the world'. While in truth they are the ones who make the world this way.

*

The birds are pecking at the tarmac for any remaining scraps. The couple has moved on. It's teatime and the veteran's carer has arrived to wheel him into the self-service café for tea and scones. The toddler, tired of making footprints in the soil, has been lifted into his buggy and is being pushed back to the car park.

I wonder about these people's lives; their pasts, their present here in the park, that toddler's future, all impossible for me to know. We comprehend so little of each other, each in our own bubble.

I get that other people haven't seen the things I've seen – most hardly give a thought to the bigger picture – but should it take a life-changing episode to see what is so obvious?

We are all here, limited in time and space, experiencing life as if we are somehow separate from each other and not part of a whole. It's a kind of optical delusion of consciousness that imprisons us inside a cage of desires, thoughts, feelings and affections for only ourselves and a very few people close to us.

We contrive to create this make-believe so we can pretend our actions don't impact on others, or even worse, so we can pretend that others are somehow less than us and therefore don't deserve the same considerations we afford ourselves. While in reality, everything we do impacts on all of us, the whole planet, for better or worse. If only we could strip away this delusion of self, everyone would be able to see the reality.

There is no them. There is only us.

We need to free ourselves by widening our circle of compassion to embrace the whole of nature in all its beauty.

Visionary thinkers like Einstein, who for me first put these thoughts into words, hope for a change of heart and mind before it's too late.

However optimistic, I've already failed to live up to my own expectations – as a community service volunteer, a housing manager and an adventure playground leader. I've tried to apply the lessons of the Light over and over again, and fallen short.

Will we ever be able to break through the delusions of this world and see things for what they really are? We would have to transform old habits, become self aware, see the Dark for what it is – the product of our own fears – and conquer our fears before anything can change. It isn't going to happen, not in my lifetime.

Underneath the ripples on the lake of human potential, still waters lie deep. I can live with that. I don't have a choice in the matter. I'm going to have to.

Sitting here alone on the bench, warmed by the sun, I feel content. In a minute I'll get up, walk to the highest hill in the park and wait for dusk. I want to watch the moon rise.

The fear of being trapped in the Dark follows me no longer. I've settled it in my mind. The first time was a terrifying unknown – I didn't have a clue where I was or if there was any way out. But my instincts kicked in. I knew I had to fight and even though I was an atheist, I knew how to call for help. If I'm unlucky and reencounter the demonic humans next time, I'll know what to expect and I hope more than anything, I'll remember how to call the Light.

I might be better prepared, but the terror of the Dark has still left its mark. It's why it's taken me so long to face up to that place, and in much the same way, it's why it's taken me twenty odd years and a life-changing experience to face up to my first deep-rooted fears.

I guess we are all terrified at some point in our childhoods by the unknown, by the dark, but while most parents are there to protect their children from fear, other parents, for whatever reasons of their own, choose to incite it.

I think of my mother following in her mother's footsteps, fearful of anything or anybody in life she can't control. And from out of her fears, finding at first relief, then pleasure in making others suffer – especially men. All this for no better reason than that's how her mother raised her. My mother wanted to escape her mother more than anything, yet she turned out just like her. The need to control is ingrained. I wonder how long this pattern of generations has existed, passed down from mother to daughter, and how long it will take to break.

I think of my grandmother. Who put the fear of God into her if not her own mother? She was terrified as much by Jehovah, the cruel and vengeful God of the Old Testament as she was by the so-called fallen angel Satan. In return for blind allegiance, the Strict and Particular Baptists had promised her eternal salvation, but when her time came, her conviction disappeared.

Eternal salvation wasn't the only gift on offer. Her church also offered free licence to punish anyone who disagreed with their doctrines, anyone not like them. Even a toddler she hated simply because he was a boy.

No matter how hard mother and daughter tried to push me down, no matter what happened in the past, I have to try and accept that in the end, both were driven by fear.

As it turns out, the Strict and Particular Baptist's version of Satan is a perversion of the original character. In the original Hebrew dialect, Satan was simply an opposer, the opposite force to the Light – something Heraclitus would've understood – put there by the old Hebrew God to test the faith of humans.

In the same way, the Grim Reaper wasn't always a terrorising ghoul stalking the living with his razor sharp scythe. As I'd learnt in the classroom, he'd started off in the mythology of Ancient Greece as a helper and assistant. Charon, the skeletal cloaked ferryman who punted the dead across the River Styx, the River of Hate, to Hades.

The price of a coin left by the living in the mouths of the dead was all it cost to pay the ferryman; for the departed to avoid drowning in the River of Hate, as I had nearly done. Over time, Christianity twisted and warped Satan and Charon out of all recognition in order to hold their congregations in fear.

*

Which leads me back to the conversation I had with Linda when we were walking in the woods. I think of all those times I'd been scared as a child; the times and places where my own fears had first taken hold. It makes me sad to think of that toddler, expecting love but not receiving it. But at least I'd discovered one thing – how to escape.

Wandering off through the exotic gardens of the Old Aged Pilgrim's Home, exploring giant forests of pampas grass, crawling into caves of rhododendron bushes, seeking refuge inside towering weeping willows; all of them friendly giants to my toddler self.

It was there in that garden I first learnt to calm my fears by discovering my love of Nature.

Mind and matter

The sun is falling out of the sky and I head for the highest hill in the park. I've been surrounded by the city for so long I need to see a horizon. Not one blocked by concrete high risers like giant letters walking across the face of the planet, but one so far away it appears to bend with the curvature of the earth.

In my attic in Portobello Road I've forgotten that over one horizon there's always another waiting to be crossed. I want to walk to the horizon, cross it and continue towards the next and the next until I've walked my dilemmas out of my system. Space goes on and on, and the further you go, the more space there is to find. What more do I need to know? Isn't that enough? I wish it was, but it isn't.

There are many mysteries left to solve and I'll just have to live with them, the same as anyone else. The more I pursue the answers, the further away they seem to move, over the next horizon and out of my reach:

The connection between the metaphysical and physical worlds and how they relate to each other.

The Source, a singularity and what this means.

Free will, and if we really do choose from a lottery of life.

The advice the Light Beings gave me about my life that, so far, I seem to have ignored.

And finally, the biggest question of all: what did the Light Beings say when I asked if we have a purpose in this world, any purpose at all? What does it mean to be the eyes and ears of the Universe?

Now is not the time to dwell on these questions. If I continue this quest, my time will be over before it's started. So I'm going to file the whole life-changing episode away and dive headfirst into the joys of life, rather than what I've been doing for far too long: drowning in the mysteries of what happens when it's all over.

I've come to an end of sorts and my map is still incomplete. For now, my rational side will have to make do with the scientific knowledge that's available. Science cannot at this moment in time answer how a mind detached from its body can exist and travel into another dimension, or how the world, so apparently solid, can disappear in a puff of smoke, like a magician's vanishing act.

Instruments haven't been invented to measure where I've been. I've explored as far as science has explored and it isn't far enough, but it's as far as I can go. I've arrived at a place where consciousness is an unknown and quantum physics is an outrage to common sense. And yet, both underpin the foundations of our modern world.

*

My own answers are more intuitive.

Solid objects, everything from mountains to amoebas to ourselves can only exist in the three-dimensional construction we call space by riding along on a fourth dimension – the crest of the tsunami – time. We live inside this stubbornly persistent illusion that there's a distinction between past, present and future while, as Einstein put it; our perception of time only exists so that everything in space doesn't happen all at once.

Outside of our space-time continuum is the metaphysical universe. How many dimensions it occupies – more or less than four – I haven't a clue. Liberated from time, space has no meaning. However many dimensions exist, they're not in another universe, they're not out there beyond Pythagoras's celestial spheres. The metaphysical world is all around us, all the time. It's in another dimension we can't see until the kernel of our consciousness is liberated from the husk of our brains. It's right here, in the eternal now, less than a millimetre away at the end of my fingertip. Just through the plaster ceiling in the hospital ward.

I reckon Dr Karim Akhtar's ideas are crucial to understanding my experience. Our brains are simply filters for an energy that's as elemental as electromagnetism – an energy called consciousness. And if our brains are filters for the outside world as he suggested, and if we sieve experiences into our minds through our brains, then what happens when we encounter an experience we can't filter? What happens when one gets stuck in the mesh?

Are these the memories, both good and bad, that remain when we die? Memories we have to re-experience before we can let them go, as I found myself doing on the way to the Light crashing through each character-defining moment? While my life flashed before my eyes and each moment disappeared, I gave up each in turn and became myself once again, a kernel of consciousness free of all attachments.

I can see how my quest hasn't only been about my beyond-death experience. It's been about my life so far and the experiences I have to let go in order to live free of my past. Because I understand now, better than most things in life, that it's the things that don't move through us that end up defining us.

*

I've been lost in thought, staring at the horizon but not really seeing it, imagining all the other horizons waiting to be crossed. Dusk has given way to night. The temperature has dropped. A shiver brings me back down to earth. The horizon line is still visible, darker than the sky above. A slither of silver breaks the line and I watch as the moon slowly rises. A giant rock hanging weightless in the sky.

As far as finding a location for the metaphysical universe goes, maybe at the end of the day, it's impossible. Perhaps it's so far beyond our quantum physical world it simply doesn't relate. It's metaphysical – otherworldly – outside of time and space entirely.

I'm no Einstein, but if the ideas I've come across about quantum physics have any relevance to my quest, then the interface between mind and matter could be located in the zero point field. That's where consciousness might be found, manifesting out of the ocean of sub-atomic particles. Waves collapse into the building blocks of our three-dimensional world. What makes them do this is a mystery, but I have a feeling it has everything to do with intention. The mystery is this: whose intention?

The quantum physicist Sir James Jeans thought that mind is not, as materialists want us to believe, a random consequence of the world of matter. Mind is actually the creator and governor of the world of matter. He wrote:

I incline to the idealistic theory that consciousness is fundamental, and that the material universe is derivative from consciousness, not consciousness from the material universe. The stream of knowledge is heading towards a non-mechanical reality;

the Universe begins to look more like a great thought than like a great machine. It may well be, it seems to me, that each individual consciousness ought to be compared to a brain-cell in a universal mind.

And in the end that, ultimately, is what it felt like to be in the Light. One single consciousness coming Home to join the myriads of others.

Other travellers

There's a knock on the front door of our house in Portobello Road and when I answer a postman hands me a cardboard package. Inside is a slim hardback book with a note that simply says, 'I hope this helps you in your search.' I know it's from Dr Karim Akhtar, though he's left no mark.

Reading the back cover, I'm transfixed. The sounds of market traders, traffic, shoppers, every intrusion from the world outside evaporates. All that's left is the book I'm holding in my hand.

It's a collection of accounts from medically verifiable sources of people who have had what the author, a doctor of philosophy, calls 'near death experiences'.

Ironically for me, I see it was published in the same year as my cardiac arrest. If only I'd known it existed, it would have broken my sense of isolation five years ago.

I flip to the start, skim the introduction and arrive at the first accounts. Over a hundred and fifty people report their fantastic journeys following cardiac arrest. Everything I experienced and more is in here.

Floating above their physical bodies, watching hospital staff trying to resuscitate them, some hearing doctors pronounce them dead, others realising it themselves. Entering a grey mist, a black void, a tunnel, or valley, the feelings of isolation.

Being drawn towards a white light, brighter than 10,000 stars but not blinding. The overwhelming feelings of love and wisdom – *every* account reports that the Light is a super-conscious being. Experiencing instant telepathic communication with the Light. Assimilating knowledge from the place where all knowledge exists. The unquestionable knowledge that this is Home.

The plastic nature of time. The flashbacks of their own lives. Reaching a border and experiencing an unwelcome return on having their bodies resuscitated.

It's an encyclopaedia of shared experiences.

Everything is here, except, that is, for the forces of the Dark. I skim through the pages. It seems impossible that so many people could have encountered the Light and yet none had seen its opposite. I come to it at the back of the book, in an addendum.

Since writing, the author has heard of people who experienced the Dark and never found their way to the Light. They had all been attempting suicide. And on their return, each and every one had regretted trying to take their own lives. The author draws on ideas in ancient theologies, which suggest that suicide is a transgression of some sort of universal rule.

I have to disagree: I found myself in the same place – but I wasn't trying to commit suicide. I died for want of a nurse to monitor my IV. My theory is that those who fall into the Dark find themselves there because they are full of fear and pain. The same fear and pain which led them to want to end their lives also happened to lead them to the Dark. I don't think that simply the act of suicide is a guarantee that you will end up in the Dark, nor do I think that any natural death will lead you straight to the Light: I fell into the Dark from lack of directions.

I wasn't prepared.

I hadn't got a map.

Well, I've got one now.

*

On their return, people's priorities changed, their outlook shifted. They found renewed interest in learning, a thirst for knowledge. They became more reflective, more considerate of others and less egotistical than before. Like myself, nobody came back with an inflated ego or any feelings of superiority or arrogance from having 'conquered' death.

In general, people felt more empathic towards others. They found it easier to see another's point of view and recognise the weaknesses of their own. No one behaved as if they thought themselves 'holier-than-thou'. On the contrary they were reticent to tell others what had happened to them. They were more reflective, considerate, and concerned with philosophical questions than they were before.

Clearly I wasn't the only one that had become an amateur philosopher after my beyond-death experience.

Almost all of the interviewees agreed about the lessons they had learnt. They stressed the importance in this life of trying to cultivate love and understanding for others; a unique and profound kind of love, devoid of any selfish or self-serving intent.

*

I feel like I've been floating alone in a life raft for five years and I've just bumped into a cruise-liner full of survivors from the same shipwreck. I share so many things in common with the people interviewed – not just the experience itself but also the after effects – the profound changes of heart and mind.

Could this be the scientific evidence I've been searching for all this time?

My father taught me that anything that can't be proved empirically by many observers, repeating the same experiment and producing the same results, simply doesn't exist. And here are the observers I've been looking for, repeating the same experiment, unwittingly like myself, but repeating it nonetheless and producing the same results again and again.

A part of me wants to rush to my parents' house and show my father the empirical proof I'm holding in my hands, but I don't. That part of me doesn't need his approval anymore and anyway, my parents are comfortable in their world. It was only me who wasn't comfortable in mine.

The book isn't a solution to my quest. As I've discovered before – crossing one horizon only to find another – the book throws up more questions than it does answers. One of them is that survivors report many more things than I'd seen myself: orbs, shining bodies, ships on a sea, fantastically beautiful landscapes full of iridescent plants and trees, cascading crystal waterfalls, flowing rivers of gold. This is more confusing than ever for the co-ordinates of my map.

Here are others who have taken the same voyage, navigated the same co-ordinates, but returned to tell a different tale. The core features are the same – the mist, the void or tunnel, the opening into the Light; most importantly the Light's universal consciousness and overwhelming love and wisdom – but each and every traveller reported their own version of what they'd found.

Why this should be, why everyone encounters a different landscape inside the Light, is a mystery. I only have my own experience to go on. It's just another piece in the puzzle, a puzzle that along with all the other missing pieces, I've accepted that I'm not going to complete. Not in this life anyway. The only solution I can fathom is that somehow the Light adopts whatever form each person finds easiest to take on board. It manifests out of their core beliefs and produces a corresponding version of itself – Nirvana, Heaven, Paradise or any number of other different landscapes. We all end up in the same metaphysical universe but each according to our nature.

If I were a Hindi, I could expect Yamaraj, a bull-headed demon with flaming hair and a club to ride in on his black buffalo and lasso my soul.

In Japan, the goddess of death Isanagi would capture me for her own, in revenge for her lost husband.

As an Australian Aborigine, and I like their take on things, Anjea the fertility goddess would pick up my soul from the sand where I'd fallen and return me to the Dreamtime, the all-at-once time where past, present and future co-exist.

And as a Buddhist I'd visit different levels of Bardo according to my karma on the way to rebirth.

Even Strict and Particular Baptists will have their own Heaven. In eternal supplication to their angry and vengeful god, Jehovah, and his forgiving son, all the time convinced that they are the only ones there.

Or as an Ancient Greek, with a coin clutched between my teeth in payment for Charon's ferry, I'd cross the River Styx, the River of Hate, unharmed, on my way to the underworld Hades.

It's taken me a long time to get here but now I've arrived the pieces of my map fall into place and it's a place I'd never have expected to find. The geography of the Light depends entirely on your own point of view.

For me, the Light adopted a universe of clouds, morphing from one thing to another. Nebulous, indeterminate and fluid in one instant and the next structured, tangible and substantial; the manifestation of a metaphysical universe seen through the lens of an atheistic teenager with a wavering scientific worldview.

I feel a little deflated about my map. The infinite variety of other people's experiences means I can only ever mark the locations of my own. The details of the geography inside the Light will be as different as the narratives of every life that enters. There is nothing definitive about the metaphysical.

But when I weigh this up I'm struck by the obvious. What was I thinking? Of course not! How can there be anything definitive in infinity?

*

I sit back and reflect on everything that's happened. When I left the space-time continuum, my geography and history unravelled. I've been searching for answers to where I went but along the way I've discovered that what my search has also been about is how to fit the pieces back together. It's taken five years but I reckon I've finally got here.

And I've learnt a little along the way. Not enough about the way of the world, about the vagaries of human nature – I guess there's plenty of time for that. But when I try and remember all the wisdom the Light showed me I feel like a dumb fool. Out of everything I learnt though, one insight remains, more important than the rest: *Only through the mind can the world be seen. Only through the heart can it be understood.* I hope this lesson will stand me in good stead.

It's time to stop putting myself in other people's shoes and start wearing my own. Time to give up my library, stop living my life inside a book and start living it in the flesh. Art College starts in the autumn. My grant has come through. I'm on my way.

Printed in Great Britain
by Amazon